Some Strange Corners
of Our Country

CHARLES F. LUMMIS

Some Strange Corners of Our Country

THE WONDERLAND OF THE SOUTHWEST

FOREWORD BY
Lawrence Clark Powell

THE UNIVERSITY OF ARIZONA PRESS
TUCSON

THE UNIVERSITY OF ARIZONA PRESS

Copyright © 1989
The Arizona Board of Regents
All Rights Reserved

♾ This book is printed on acid-free, archival-quality paper.
Manufactured in the United States of America
93 92 91 90 89   5 4 3 2 1
Library of Congress Cataloging-in-Publication Data

Lummis, Charles Fletcher, 1859–1928.
    Some strange corners of our country : the wonderland of the
Southwest / Charles F. Lummis ; foreword by Lawrence Clark Powell.
        p.   cm.
    Reprint. Previously published: New York : Century Co., 1898.
    ISBN 0-8165-0852-6 (alk. paper)
    1. Southwest, New — Description and travel.   2. Natural history —
Southwest, New.   I. Title.
F786.L945   1989
917.9'042 — dc19   88-26703
                                                                    CIP

British Library Cataloguing in Publication data are available.

TO MY WIFE: WHO HAS
SHARED THE HARDSHIPS AND
THE PLEASURES OF EXPLORING
THE STRANGE CORNERS

CONTENTS

LIST OF ILLUSTRATIONS

FOREWORD

LAWRENCE CLARK POWELL

 E set out alone on foot, September 11, 1884, to walk from Ohio to California — and he made it, arriving in Los Angeles the next year on the first of February. By another ten years he had become the greatest booster the Southwest has ever known.

This Yankee maverick was Charles Fletcher Lummis, called Lum, the son of a Massachusetts minister, not quite a Harvard graduate, having withdrawn just before Commencement when trouble with two women threatened to fence him in. He fathered a daughter by one and married the other, then left her in Cambridge to finish her medical degree while he headed for Ohio to work on her father's farm. He soon found something better as editor of the *Scioto Gazette*. Young Lum always managed to land on his feet and running.

He needed something to settle him down. With a gift for writing first apparent at Harvard and developed while on the Chillicothe newspaper, Lummis struck a long-distance deal with General Harrison Gray Otis, owner of the *Los*

Angeles Times, that would take him on that long walk, filing dispatches of his adventures along the way. He had plenty of them — at least he said so.

And so he set out for what promised to be a better land and job. News had reached the East of what became known as the Boom of the Eighties in Southern California. It was the craziest time since the Gold Rush. His route was the Old Santa Fe Trail, followed by traders and travelers since the 1820s, and now by the new railroad to the coast.

Unlike the argonauts, Lummis did not challenge the Rockies, taking instead the low road to Santa Fe. Like those before him, he marveled at sight of the battlements, "shutting the whole western sky from north to south, far as sight could reach, distant, severe and cold."

That turn in the road was the most meaningful ever taken by Lummis, for it led to a lifelong commitment to a land of "Sun, Silence and Adobe." Not only did he discover a newfoundland, he was met there by warm and welcoming people whose skin was a different color from his. We all start with racial prejudice, he was to say, and few graduate from it. He was one who did, as he became an eloquent champion of the inhabitants, Indian and Spanish. He was also the first to christen that land The Southwest and to coin the phrase See America First.

In Santa Fe, letters of introduction led to Amado Chavez, scion of an old New Mexican family and Speaker of the territorial House of Representatives. He soon pressed on west, visiting the Chavez domain at the foot of Mt. Taylor, easternmost sacred peak of the Navajos. There he formed a lasting bond with that family. His first son, lost to death at six, was named Amado.

In Southern California, Lummis had another unexpected welcome when he was met at the Los Angeles city limits by General Otis himself and given the job of city editor of the *Times*. After five hectic years, including coverage of Geronimo's uprising and failure to become a good husband to his wife Dorothea, now practicing medicine in Los Angeles, Lummis took refuge in a paralytic stroke that crippled his left side.

He recuperated on the Chavez hacienda at San Mateo, then went to live with the Tewa Indians at Isleta Pueblo, on the Rio Grande below Albuquerque. There he was nursed back to health by the mission's schoolteacher, Eva Frances Douglas. Despite Dr. Dorothea's efforts to hold him, Lummis gained his freedom to marry the younger woman. In an unusual act of thanks, he dedicated his book, *Land of Poco Tiempo*, "To Eva and Dorothea."

Once again he began to write to make a living, eastern magazines his market, the Southwest his subject. In those early years of the transcontinental railroad, what became the Santa Fe found it good business to give Lummis a pass on either Pullman or caboose.

He was thus able to make several trips to New York, where he lunched with such literary arbiters as Richard Watson Gilder and Brander Matthews. At Tiffany's he offered to show their jewels on the bridle of his horse Alazan. The Harvard connection did him no harm. Now a western eccentric, he paid a Manhattan tailor twenty-five dollars to make him a three-piece suit of corduroy, henceforth his standard apparel, sometimes topped with an Indian headband and a red sash around his waist.

During the early 1890s Lummis exploded with articles, all

celebrating his new land. From 1891 to 1894 they were gathered in six solid volumes. This honeymoon harvest marked his high point as a promoter of the Southwest. Although he lived until 1928, based in Los Angeles, and never stopped fighting for the preservation of our cultural past, Lummis did not surpass that burst of books.

Now a century later, while civilization has come to every corner, it has not changed the wonders celebrated in *Some Strange Corners of Our Country*. Therein Lummis fixed the vision and configuration of an Enchanted Land. Thirty years later when he haltingly enlarged that book into *Mesa, Cañon and Pueblo*, the freshness was gone. The result was heavy, the updating outdated. His publisher had to nag him to finish; his heart was not in it.

In that one halcyon time, newly married and father of a growing family, Lummis flowered. The pressures of being celebrated and controversial lay ahead, and he led a carefree if Spartan existence, living on wild fruits and on jam and doughnuts of his own making. His unpublished journal of those three and a half years at Isleta are rich with incidents of his daily life not included in his books, such as a glimpse of a 400-pound Indian grandmother whose job was to sit over the place in the floor beneath which the family's gold was buried. Some ties with Isleta lasted the rest of his life, when the young sons of his old friends came to Los Angeles to help him build El Alisal, the great stone house on the bank of the Arroyo Seco.

Among those early books, *Some Strange Corners of Our Country* remains one of the best, as sound as ever in knowledge and strong in feeling. Although published by Century, most of its chapters first appeared in *St. Nicholas* magazine. Its bold illustrations were replaced in the later volume by pallidly reproduced photographs taken by the author. Not until 1987 were his Pueblo documentary views well printed.

Thanks to preservation of those natural wonders as national parks and monuments — first urged by Lummis — today's visitors to the Southwest will find this book a useful companion. The land is still there in all its immensity: the Grand Canyon has been saved from further damming, although its sky is noisy with aircraft; Montezuma Well still flows into Beaver Creek through a crack in the limestone, while Montezuma Castle stands guard; the Petrified Forest, Tonto Bridge, and the Lava Flow have been preserved; and Inscription Rock, safeguarded in 1906 by President Theodore Roosevelt, Lummis's Harvard schoolmate, still emerges from the low piñon-juniper forest as El Morro National Monument. All is still there, timelessly pristine.

That is why this first look, with an understanding of what is seen, is worth reprinting. It endures as one of the lasting achievements of this first and best popularizer of the Southwest.

SOME STRANGE CORNERS OF OUR COUNTRY.

I.

THE GRANDEST GORGE IN THE WORLD.

WE live in the most wonderful of lands; and one of the most wonderful things in it is that we as Americans find so little to wonder at. Other civilized nations take pride in knowing their points of natural and historic interest; but when we have pointed to our marvelous growth in population and wealth, we are very largely done, and hasten abroad in quest of sights not a tenth part so wonderful as a thousand wonders we have at home and never dream of. It is true that other nations are older, and have grown up to think of something besides material matters; but our youth and our achievements are poor excuse for this unpatriotic slighting

of our own country. There is a part of America,—a part
even of the United States—of which Americans know as
little as they do of inner Africa, and of which too many of
them are much less interested to learn. With them "to
travel" means only to go abroad; and they call a man a
traveler who has run his superficial girdle around the world
and is as ignorant of his own country (except its cities) as if
he had never been in it. I hope to live to see Americans
proud of *knowing America,* and ashamed not to know it; and
it is to my young countrymen that I look for the patriotism
to effect so needed a change.

If we would cease to depend so much upon other countries
for our models of life and thought, we would have taken the
first step toward the Americanism which should be, but is
not, ours. We read a vast amount of the wonders of foreign
lands; but very few writers—and still fewer reliable ones—
tell us of the marvelous secrets of our own. Every intelligent
youth knows that there are boomerang-throwers in Australia;
but how many are aware that there are thousands of aborigines in the United States just as expert with the magic club
as are the Bushmen?* All have read of the astounding feats
of the jugglers of India; but how many know that there are
as good Indian jugglers within our own boundaries? The
curious "Passion Play" at Oberammergau is in the knowledge of most young Americans; but very few of them have
learned the startling fact that every year sees in the United

* The Pueblo Indians, who annually kill countless thousands of rabbits with these weapons.

THE GRAND CAÑON OF THE COLORADO. GENERAL VIEW.

States an infinitely more dramatic Passion *Reality,*—a flesh
and blood crucifixion,—wherein an ignorant fanatic represents *in fact* the death of the Savior. How many young
Americans could say, when some traveler recounted the ex-
ploits of the world-famous snake-charmers of the Orient,
"Why, yes, we have tribes of Indians in this country whose
trained charmers handle the deadliest snakes with impunity,"
and go on to tell the astonishing facts in the case? How
many know that there are Indians here who dwell in huge
six-story tenements of their own building? How many know
that the last witch in the United States did not go up in the
cruel smoke of old Salem, but that there is still within our
borders a vast domain wherein witchcraft is as fully believed
in as yesterday is, and where somebody is executed every
year for the strange crime of "being a witch"?

These are but a few of the strange things at home of
which we know not. There are thousands of others; and if
it shall ever become as fashionable to write about America
as it is about Africa, we shall have chance to learn that in
the heart of the most civilized nation on earth are still savage peoples, whose customs are stranger and more interesting than those of the Congo.

As to our scenery, we are rather better informed; and
yet every year thousands of un-American Americans go to
Europe to see scenery infinitely inferior to our own, upon
which they have never looked. We say there are no ruins in
this country, and cross the ocean to admire crumbling piles
less majestic and less interesting than are in America. We

ANOTHER VIEW OF THE GRAND CAÑON.

read of famous gorges and defiles abroad, and are eager to
see them, unknowing that in a desolate corner of the United
States is the greatest natural wonder of the world—a cañon
in which all the world's *famous* gorges could be lost forever.
And not one American in ten thousand has ever looked upon
its awful grandeur.

Of course, we know the Sahara, for that is not American;
but you will seek far to find any one who is familiar with an
American desert as absolute and as fearful.　We are aware
of our giant redwoods in California,—the hugest trees in
the world,—but did you ever hear of a petrified forest covering thousands of acres?　There is one such in the United
States, and many smaller ones.　Do you know that in one
territory alone we have the ruins of over fifteen hundred
stone cities as old as Columbus, and many of them far older?
Have you ever heard of towns here whose houses are three-
story caves, hewn from the solid rock?

It seems to me that when these and so many other wonders are a part of America, we, who are Americans, should
be ashamed to know absolutely nothing of them.　If such
things existed in England or Germany or France, there
would be countless books and guides overflowing with infor-
mation about them, and we would hasten on excursions to
them, or learn all that reading would tell us.

There is no untruer proverb than the one which says, "It
is never too late to learn."　As we grow old we learn many
things, indeed, and fancy ourselves enormously wise; but
that wisdom is only the skin of life, so to say, and what we

learn in youth is the real bone and blood. I would rather interest one of my young countrymen than a thousand of the unconvertible older ones; and if I could induce him to resolve that, whatever else he learned, he would learn all he could of his own country, I should be very happy indeed. Let me tell you briefly, then, of a few of the strange corners of our country which I have found—something of the wonderland of the southwest—which I hope you will some day be interested to see for yourselves.

I have spoken of the Grand Cañon of the Colorado as a gorge in which all the *famous* gorges could be lost. Some of you have ridden through the "Grand Cañon of the Arkansaw," on the Denver and Rio Grande Railway in Colorado, and still more through the White Mountain Notch and the Franconia Notch in New Hampshire. All three are very beautiful and noble; but if any one of them were duplicated in the wall of the Grand Cañon of the Colorado, and you were looking from the opposite brink of that stupendous chasm, you would have to have your attention called to those scratches on the other side before you would notice them at all! If you were to take the tallest mountain east of the Rockies, dig down around its base a couple of thousand feet so as to get to the sea-level (from which its height is measured), uproot the whole giant mass, and pitch it into the deepest of the Grand Cañon of the Colorado, its granite top would not reach up to the dizzy crests of the cliffs which wall the awful bed of that muddy river. If you were on the stream, and New York's noble statue of Liberty Enlighten-

WITHIN THE GRAND CAÑON.

ing the World were upon the cliff, it would look to you like
the tiniest of dolls; and if it were across the cañon from
you, you would need a strong glass to see it at all!

The Grand Cañon lies mostly in Arizona, though it touches
also Utah, Nevada, and California. With its windings and
side-cañons of the first magnitude it is nearly seven hundred
miles long; and in many places it is over a mile and a quarter deep! The width of this unparalleled chasm at the top
is from eight to twenty miles; and looked down upon from
above, a larger river than the Hudson (and more than three
times as long) looks like a silver thread. The Yosemite and
the Yellowstone, wonderful as they are in their precipices,—
and the world outside of America cannot match those wondrous valleys,—are babies beside this peerless gorge.

The walls of the Grand Cañon are in most places not perpendicular; but seen from in front they all appear to be.
They are mostly of sandstone, but in places of marble, and
again of limestone, and yet again of volcanic rock; generally
"terraced" in a manner entirely peculiar to the southwest,
and cleft into innumerable buttes, which seem towers and
castles, but are infinitely more vast and more noble than the
hand of man will ever rear. And when the ineffable sun-
shine of that arid but enchanted land falls upon their wondrous domes and battlements with a glow which seems not
of this world, the sight is such a revelation that I have seen
strong men sit down and weep in speechless awe.

There are no great falls in the Grand Cañon; but many
beautiful and lofty ones in the unnumbered hundreds of side-

HEAD OF THE GRAND CAÑON OF THE COLORADO.

cañons which en-
ter the great one.
I had almost said
"little cañons,"
for so they seem
in the presence
of their giant
mother; but in
reality, almost
any one of them
would shame any
cañon elsewhere.

There is no
such thing as
describing the
Grand Cañon,
and I dare not
try. But I shall
borrow a few
words from the
man who has
come nearer giv-
ing in words a
hint of the cañon
than has any one
else — Charles
Dudley Warner.
He has said:

2

CLIMBING IN THE GRAND CAÑON.

"This region is probably the most interesting territory of its size on the globe. At least it is unique. In attempting to convey an idea of it the writer can be assisted by no comparison. . . . The Vermilion Cliffs, the Pink Cliffs, the White Cliffs surpass in fantastic form and brilliant color anything that the imagination conceives possible in nature; and there are dreamy landscapes quite beyond the most exquisite fancies of Claude and of Turner. The region is full of wonders, of beauties, and sublimities that Shelley's imaginings do not match in the 'Prometheus Unbound.' . . . Human experience has no prototype of this region, and the imagination has never conceived of its forms and colors. It is impossible to convey an adequate idea of it by pen or pencil or brush. . . . The whole magnificence broke upon us. No one could be prepared for it. The scene is one to strike dumb with awe, or to unstring the nerves. . . . It was a shock so novel that the mind, dazed, quite failed to comprehend it. All that we could comprehend was a vast confusion of amphitheaters and strange architectural forms resplendent with color. The vastness of the view amazed us quite as much as its transcendent beauty. . . . We had come into a new world. . . . This great space is filled with gigantic architectural constructions, with amphitheaters, gorges, precipices, walls of masonry, fortresses, temples mountain size, all brilliant with horizontal lines of color—streaks of solid hues a thousand feet in width—yellows, mingled white and gray, orange, dull red, brown, blue, carmine, green, all blending in the sunlight into one transcendent effusion of splendor. . . .

ANOTHER VIEW OF THE GRAND CAÑON.

The vast abyss has an atmosphere of its own . . . golden, rosy, gray, brilliant and somber, and playing a thousand fantastic tricks to the vision. . . . Some one said that all that was needed to perfect this scene was a Niagara Falls. I thought what figure a fall 150 feet high and 3000 long would make in this arena. It would need a spy-glass to discover it. An adequate Niagara here should be at least three miles in breadth and fall 2000 feet over one of those walls. And the Yosemite—ah! the lovely Yosemite! Dumped down into this wilderness of gorges and mountains, it would take a guide who knew of its existence a long time to find it. . . . Those who have long and carefully studied the Grand Cañon of the Colorado do not hesitate for a moment to pronounce it by far the most sublime of all earthly spectacles."

Very few Americans see the Grand Cañon—shamefully few. Most of it lies in an absolute desert, where are neither people, food, nor obtainable water—for the river has carved this indescribable abyss of a trough through a vast flat upland, from which in many places a descent to the stream is impossible; and yet the cañon is easily reached at some points. The Atlantic and Pacific Railroad comes (at Peach Springs, Arizona) within twenty-three miles of it, and one can take a stage to the cañon. The stage-road winds down to the bottom of the Grand Cañon by way of the Diamond Creek Cañon, which is itself a wonderful chasm.

The point whence Mr. Warner saw the cañon was at the head of the Hance trail, in the Kaibab plateau; and it is by far the sublimest part of the cañon that is accessible. It is reached by a sixty-seven-mile ride from Flagstaff on the Atlantic and Pacific Railroad. Three hundred and fifty years ago a poor Spanish lieutenant with twenty men penetrated that fearful wilderness and looked down upon the world's utmost wonder. And only now, for the first time in its history, is the Grand Cañon easily accessible to the traveler at its noblest point. A good stage-line has just been started from Flagstaff, and I went out on the second trip, unwilling to advise travelers except from personal knowledge. Mr. Clarke, of St. Nicholas, was with me. The road has been much improved since Mr. Warner's visit, and is now the best long mountain-road in the southwest. There are comfortable hotels in Flagstaff, the stages are comfortable, the three relays of horses make the sixty-seven-mile journey easily in eleven hours, and there is nothing in the trip to deter ladies or young people. The drive is through the fine pine forests, with frequent and changing views of the noble San Francisco peaks and the Painted Desert. It brings one to the very brink of this terrific gorge almost without warning; and one looks down suddenly upon all that matchless wonderland. The cañon is here 6600 feet deep. One can explore it for miles along the rim, finding new wonders at every step. Even if one sits in one spot, one sees a new cañon every hour —the scene-changers are always shifting that divine stage-setting. One should not fail to descend the excellent trail to the river—seven miles—built by that interesting pioneer John Hance. It gives an altogether new idea of the cañon —and if one stays a month and travels every hour of daylight, one does not yet realize the cañon. At the end of a lifetime, it would be more interesting than ever.

The stage journey takes a day each way, and the fare for the round trip is twenty dollars. One should take as much time as possible at the cañon; but three days in all (including the stage-ride) is better than nothing—indeed, is better than anything anywhere else. Good meals and beds are there at one dollar each. This line can operate only from May 1st to December 1st, on account of the winter snows of that 7000-foot plateau; but from December to May one can go in by the Peach Springs route, which reaches the bottom of the cañon, and is more comfortable in winter than in summer.

II.

A FOREST OF AGATE.

ROM the Atlantic and Pacific Railroad it is still easier to reach a great natural curiosity — the huge Petrified Forest of Arizona. Much the nearest point is the little station of Billings, but there are scant accommodations there for the traveler — only a railroad section-house and a ranch-house. Only a mile south of the track, at that point, one may see a low, dark ridge, marked by a single cotton-wood tree. Walking thither (over a valley so alive with jack-rabbits that there is some excuse for the cow-boy declaration that "you can walk clear across on their backs!") one soon reaches the northern edge of the forest, which covers hundreds of square miles. Unless you are more hardened to wonderful sights than I am, you will almost fancy yourself in some enchanted spot. You seem to stand on the glass of a gigantic kaleidoscope, over whose sparkling surface the sun breaks in infinite rainbows. You are ankle-deep in such chips as I 'll warrant you never saw from any other woodpile. What do you think of chips from trees that are red moss-agate, and amethyst, and smoky topaz, and agate of every hue? That is exactly the sort of splinters that cover the ground for miles here, around the huge prostrate trunks—some of them five feet through—from which Time's patient ax has hewn them. I broke a specimen from the heart of a tree there, years ago, which had, around the stone pith, a remarkable array of large and exquisite crystals; for on one side of the specimen—which is not so large as my hand—is a beautiful mass of crystals of royal purple amethyst, and on the other an equally beautiful array of smoky topaz crystals. One can also get magnificent cross-sections of a whole trunk, so thin as to be portable, and showing every vein and even the bark. There is not a chip in all those miles which is not worthy a place, just as it is, in the proudest cabinet, and when polished I know no other rock so splendid. It is one of the hardest stones in the world, and takes and keeps an incomparable polish.

In the curious sandstone hills a mile northeast of Billings is an outlying part of the forest, less beautiful but fully as strange. There you will find giant petrified logs, three and four feet in diameter, projecting yards from steep bluffs of a peculiar bluish clay. Curiously enough, *this* "wood" is not agate, nor bright-hued, but a soft combination of browns and grays, and absolutely opaque—whereas all the "wood" across the valley is translucent and some of it quite transparent. It also "splits up" in an entirely different fashion. But if these half-hidden logs in the bluffs are less attractive to the eye, they are quite as interesting, for they tell even more clearly of the far, forgotten days when all this great upland (now five thousand feet above the sea) sank with all

its forests, and lay for centuries in water strongly charged
with mineral, which turned the undecaying trees to eternal
stone.   These latter trunks project about a third of the way
up a bluff over one hundred feet high.   They are packed in a
twenty-foot deposit of fine clay; and above them since the
waters buried them there has formed a stratum of solid sandstone more than thirty feet thick!   That shows what uncounted millenniums they have been there.   The erosion
which has carved the bluffs out of the general table-land,
and thus at last exposed the ends of these stone logs, was of
comparatively recent date.   There is no knowing how much
more earth and stone lay once above the logs, when erosion
first began to change the face of the whole country.   Other
logs are solidly imbedded in the rock cliff itself.

The most convenient way of reaching the Petrified Forest
—and the most impressive part of it—is by a fifteen-mile
drive from Holbrook station.   In Chalcedony Park, as this
part of the forest is called, is the largest number of huge petrified trees to be found in any one place in the world.   One
of them spans a deep arroyo forty feet wide, forming probably the only bridge of solid agate on this globe.   The inev-
itable vandal has blown up a few of these superb stone logs
with giant-powder, to get some specimens for his contempt-
ible pocket; but there are thousands still spared, and the
forest is now so guarded that a repetition of these outrages
is not probable.   In Tiffany's jewelry store, New York, you
can see some magnificent specimens of polished cross-sections
from these logs, which command enormous prices.   The man

TREE-TRUNK PETRIFIED INTO AN AGATE BRIDGE.

in Sioux Falls who superintended the sawing of them told me that a steel saw, six inches wide and aided by diamond-dust, was worn down to a half-inch ribbon in going through thirty-six inches of that adamantine "wood"—a process which lasted many days.

This petrified forest was a very important thing in the economy of the brown first Americans—long centuries before Europe dreamed of a New World. Its beautiful "woods" traveled all over the great southwest, and sometimes far out into the plains. Not that the Indians used it for jewelry as we are now doing; but they made of it articles far more valuable than the little charms into which it is nowadays polished by the thousands of dollars' worth annually. Some of this agate was the very best material possible for their arrow-heads, spear-heads, knives, scrapers, and other material; and they seem to have preferred it to the commoner volcanic glass. Many hundreds of miles from the Petrified Forest I have picked up these stone implements which were unmistakably made from its "wood." I have hundreds of beautiful arrow-points, and many spear-heads of all sorts of agate, and several scalping-knives of lovely moss agate, all of which came from there originally, though all found at long distances away. The Indians used to make excursions thither to get these prized chips; and evidently traded them to very distant tribes.

In the extreme eastern edge of Arizona, some forty miles southeast of the Petrified Forest, and about forty miles southwest of the remote and interesting Indian pueblo of Zuñi,

3

N. M., is a strange natural phenomenon — a great, shallow salt lake, at the bottom of a bowl-like depression some hundreds of feet deep and about three miles across. The basin is daz-zling white with a crust of salt crystals. About in the center rises a small black volcanic peak; and if you will take the trouble to ford the salt lake — which is disagreeable but not dangerous to do — and climb the peak, you will find its crater half-filled with a lakelet of pure, fresh water ! There are very many of these salt lakes in the southwest, and from them the Indians from time immemorial have procured their salt — and so did the Mexican colonists until within ten years. There is also a large river of salt water — the Salt River, in south-western Arizona.

A very curious and disagreeable freak of nature found in some parts of the southwest is that treacherous pitfall known as the *sumidero*. These ugly traps are quite numerous in some valleys — particularly in the vicinity of San Mateo, N. M. There is no danger-signal to show their whereabouts; and the first warning one has of a *sumidero* is apt to be too late. These characteristic pits are a sort of mud springs with too much mud to flow, and too much water to dry up. They are roundish, about the size of a well-hole, and some-times as deep — in fact, they are what we might call masked wells. There are quicksands at various points in nearly every stream of the southwest; but even these, frequently fatal as they are, are not nearly so dangerous as the *sumideros*. In fording a southwestern stream one expects, and is prepared for, quicksands. But there is no looking out for a *sumidero*.

These masked wells occur in bare, alkali-covered flats. The mud upon their surface is baked dry, and there is absolutely nothing to distinguish them from the safe ground around. But man or horse or sheep or cow that once steps upon that treacherous surface slumps from sight in an instant. Many animals and some people perish in these *sumideros*, and the bodies are hardly ever recovered. The longest pole will not find bottom to one of these mud springs. A Mexican friend of mine is one of the few who ever got into a *sumidero* and got out again. He was loping across the dry plain when suddenly the horse disappeared in a great splash of mud. The rider was thrown from the saddle, and clutched the edges of the pit so that he was able to draw himself out.

The pueblo of Zuñi itself is well worthy of a visit. It has an important history, as you will see in the chapter on the Stone Autograph Album; and its architecture, its people, and its customs are full of keen interest to every intelligent American. Among the least of its curiosities are several blonde Indians as genuine albinos as white rabbits are. They are pure-blooded Indians, but their skins are very light, their hair almost tow-color, and their eyes red. The people of Zuñi also make the handsomest pottery of all the Pueblos; and some of their large old water-jars, painted with strange figures of elk and other animals, are really valuable. The best way to get to Zuñi is from the station of Gallup, where carriages and drivers can be procured. The road is too easily lost for the stranger to undertake it alone; but the tireless horses of the country cover the lonely miles in a few hours.

III.

HE Great American Desert was almost better known a generation ago than it is to-day. Then thousands of the hardy Argonauts had traversed that fearful waste on foot with their dawdling ox-teams, and hundreds of them had left their bones to bleach in that thirsty land. The survivors of those deadly journeys had a very definite idea of what that desert was; but now that we can roll across it in a day in Pullman palace-cars, its real—and still existing—horrors are largely forgotten. I have walked its hideous length alone and wounded, and realize something more of it from that than a great many railroad journeys across it since have told me. Now every transcontinental railroad crosses the great desert whose vast, arid waste stretches up and down the continent, west of the Rocky Mountains, for nearly two thousand miles. The northern routes cut its least gruesome parts; but the two which traverse its southern half—the Atlantic and Pacific Railroad and the Southern Pacific Railroad— pierce some of its grimmest recesses.

The first scientific exploration of this deadly area was Lieutenant Wheeler's United States survey in the early fifties; and

THE GREAT AMERICAN DESERT. (FROM A PHOTOGRAPH.)

he was first to give scientific assurance that we have here a desert as absolute as the Sahara. If its parched sands could speak their record, what a story they might tell of unearthly sufferings and raving death; of slow-plodding caravans, whose patient oxen lifted their feet ceaselessly from the blistering gravel and bawled with agony; of drawn human faces that peered hungrily at yon lying image of a placid lake, and toiled frantically on to sink at last, hopeless and strengthless, in the hot dust which the mirage had painted with the hues and the very waves of water; and whose were the ghastly relics that whiten there to-day, uncrumbled after a generation of exposure to the dryest air on the globe!

No one will ever know how many have laid their gaunt forms to the long sleep in that inhospitable land; but the number runs up into the thousands. Not a year passes, even now, without record of many deaths upon that desert, and of many more who wander back, crazed with the delirium of thirst, and are taken to a kindlier clime only to die there. Even people at the railroad stations sometimes rove off, lured by the strange fascination of the desert, and never come back; and of the adventurous miners who seek to probe the golden secrets of those barren and strange-hued ranges, there are countless victims.

A desert is not necessarily an endless, level waste of burning sand; and the Great American Desert is far from it. It is full of strange, burnt, ragged mountain ranges, with deceptive, sloping broad valleys between — though as we near its southern end the mountains become somewhat less nu-

merous, and the sandy wastes more prominent. There are
countless extinct volcanoes upon it, and hundreds of square
miles of black, bristling lava-flows. A majority of it is
sparsely clothed with the hardy greasewood; but in places
not a plant of any sort breaks the surface, far as the eye can
reach. The summer heat is inconceivable, often reaching
136° in the shade; and a piece of metal which has lain in
the sun can no more be handled than could a red-hot stove.
Even in winter the midday heat is sometimes insufferable,
while at night ice frequently forms on the water-tanks.   The
daily range of temperature there is said to be the greatest
ever recorded anywhere; and a change of 80° in a few hours
is not rare.   Such violent variations are extremely trying to
the human system; and among the few people who live on
the edges of the hottest of lands, pneumonia is the commonest
of diseases! The scattered telegraph-offices along the railroad are all built with two roofs, a couple of feet apart, that
the free passage of air may partially counteract the fearful
down-beating of the sun.   There are oases in the desert, too,
chief of which are the narrow valleys of the Mojave River
and the lower Colorado.   It is a strange thing to see that
soft green ribbon athwart the molten landscape—between
lines as sharp-drawn as a fence, on one side of which all is
verdant life, and on the other, but a foot away, all death and
desolation.

The contorted ranges, which seem to have been dropped
down upon the waste, rather than upheaved from it, are very
rich in gold and silver,—a fact which has lured countless

victims to death. Their strange colors have given an appropriate name to one of the largest silver-producing districts
in the United States—that of Calico. The curiously blended
browns and reds of these igneous rocks do make them
strongly resemble the antiquated calicoes of our grand-
mothers.

As would be inferred from its temperature, the desert is a
land of fearful winds. When that stupendous volume of hot
air rises by its own lightness—as hot air always must rise, a
principle which was the foundation of ballooning—other air
from the surrounding world must rush in to take its place;
and as the new ocean of atmosphere, greater than the Medi-
terranean, pours in in stupendous waves to its desert bed,
such winds result as few in fertile lands ever dreamed of.
The Arabian simoom is not deadlier than the sand-storm of
the Colorado Desert (as the lower half is generally called).
Express-trains cannot make head against it—nay, they are
even sometimes forced from the track! Upon the crests of
some of the ranges are hundreds of acres buried deep in the
fine, white sand that those fearful gales pluck up by car-loads
from the plain and lift on high to fling upon the scowling
peaks thousands of feet above. There are no snow-drifts to
blockade trains there; but it is sometimes necessary to shovel
through more troublesome drifts of sand. Man or beast
caught in one of those sand-laden tempests has little chance
of escape. The man who will lie with his head tightly
wrapped in coat or blanket and stifle there until the fury of
the storm is spent may survive; but woe to the poor brute

whose swift feet cannot bear it betimes to a place of refuge.
There is no facing or breathing that atmosphere of alkaline
sand, whose lightest whiff inflames eyes, nose, and throat
almost past endurance.   The sand-storm suffocates its vic-

VIEW AMONG THE CACTI.

tims and buries them—perhaps to uncover them again only
after the lapse of years.

The few rivers of the American Desert are as strange and
as treacherous as its winds.   The Colorado is the only large
stream of them all, and the only one which behaves like an
ordinary river.   It is always turbid—and gets its Spanish

name, which means "the Red," from the color of its tide. The smaller streams are almost invariably clear in dry weather; but in a time of rain they become torrents not so much of sandy water as of liquid sand! I have seen them rolling down in freshets with four-foot waves which seemed simply sand in flow; and it is a fact that the bodies of those who are drowned at such times are almost never recovered. The strange river buries them forever in its own sands. All these rivers have heads; but hardly one of them has a mouth! They rise in the mountains on the edge of some happier land, flow away out into the desert, making a green gladness where their waters touch, and soon are swallowed up forever by the thirsty sands. The Mojave, for instance, is a beautiful little stream, clear as crystal through the summer, only a foot or so in depth, but a couple of hundred feet wide. It is fifty or sixty miles long, and its upper valley is a narrow paradise, green with tall grasses and noble cotton-woods that recall the stately elms of the Connecticut Valley. But lower down the grass gives place to barren sand-banks; the hardier trees, whose roots bore deep to drink, grow small and straggling; and at last it dies altogether upon the arid plain, and leaves beyond a desert as utter as that which crowds its whole bright oasis-ribbon on either side but cannot encroach thereon.

It is a very curious fact that this American Sahara, over fifteen hundred miles long from north to south, and nearly half as wide, serves to trip the very seasons. On its one side the rains all come in the summer; but on the Pacific side

they are invariably in the winter, and a shower between
March and October is almost as unheard of as the prover-
bial thunder from a cloudless sky.

In the southern portions of the desert are many strange
freaks of vegetable life—huge cacti sixty feet tall, and as
large around as a barrel, with singular arms which make
them look like gigantic candelabra; smaller but equally fantastic varieties of cactus, from the tall, lithe *ocalilla*, or whip-
stock cactus, down to the tiny knob smaller than a china cup,
whose innocent-looking needles give it a roseate halo.   The
blossoms of these strange vegetable pin-cushions (whose pins
all have their points outward) are invariably brilliant and
beautiful.   There are countless more modest flowers, too, in
the rainy season, and thousands of square miles are carpeted
thick with a floral carpet which makes it hard for the traveler to believe that he is really gazing upon a desert.   There
are even date-palms, those quaint ragged children of the trop-
ics; and they have very appropriate company.   Few people
are aware that there are wild camels in North America, but
it is none the less true.   Many years ago a number of these
"ships of the desert" were imported from Africa by an en-
terprising Yankee who purposed to use them in freighting
across the American Sahara.   The scheme failed; the camels
escaped to the desert, made themselves at home, and there
they roam to-day, wild as deer but apparently prospering,
and now and then frightening the wits nearly out of some
ignorant prospector who strays into their grim domain.

There are in this desert weird and deadly valleys which

are hundreds of feet below the level of the sea; vast deposits of pure salt, borax, soda, and other minerals; remarkable "mud-volcanoes," or geysers; wonderful mirages and supernatural atmospheric effects, and many other wonders. The intensely dry air is so clear that distance seems annihilated, and the eye loses its reckoning. Objects twenty miles away look to be within an easy half-hour's walk. There are countless dry beds of prehistoric and accursed lakes—some of them of great extent—in whose alkaline dust no plant can grow, and upon which a puddle of rain-water becomes an almost deadly poison. In the mountain-passes are trails where the pattering feet of mangy and starveling coyotes for thousands of years have worn a path six inches deep in the solid limestone. Gaunt ravens sail staring over the wan plains; and hairy tarantulas hop; and the side-winder—the deadly, horned rattlesnake of the desert, which gets its nickname from its peculiar sideling motion—crawls across the burning sands, or basks in the terrific sun which only he and the lizards, of all created things, can enjoy.

The "Salton Sea," about which so much undeserved sensation and mystery were made recently, is not a sea at all, but a huge puddle of "back water" from the Colorado River. It had been dry for a great while; but the river in 1891, in a freshet, broke its banks and again filled the shallow basin. The water is brackish because the overflowed valley contains great salt deposits.

The most fatally famous part of the Great American Desert is Death Valley, in California. There is on all the

4

globe no other spot so forbidding, so desolate, so deadly.   It is a concentration of the hideousness of that whole hideous area; and it has a bitter history.

One of the most interesting and graphic stories I ever listened to was that related to me, several years ago, by one of the survivors of the famous Death Valley party of 1849 — Rev. J. W. Brier, an aged Methodist clergyman now living in California, who preached the first Protestant sermon in Los Angeles. A party of five hundred emigrants started on the last day of September, 1849, from the southern end of Utah to cross the desert to the new mines of California. There were one hundred and five canvas-topped wagons, drawn by sturdy oxen, beside which trudged the shaggy men, rifle in hand, while under the canvas awnings rode the women and children.   In a short time there was division of opinion as to the proper route across that pathless waste in front; and next day five wagons and their people went east to reach Santa Fé (whence there were dim Mexican trails to Los Angeles), and the rest plunged boldly into the desert. The party which went *via* Santa Fé reached California in December, after vast sufferings.   The larger company traveled in comfort for a few days until they reached about where Pioche now is.   Then they entered the Land of Thirst; and for more than three months wandered lost in that inconceivable realm of horror.   It was almost impossible to get wagons through a country furrowed with cañons; and presently they abandoned their vehicles, packing what they could upon the backs of the oxen.   They struggled on to glittering lakes,

only to find them deadly poison, or but a mirage on barren
sands. Now and then a wee spring in the mountains gave
them new life. One by one the oxen dropped, day by day
the scanty flour ran lower. Nine young men, who separated
from the rest, being stalwart and unencumbered with fami-

REV. J. W. BRIER.

lies, strayed into Death Valley ahead of the others, succumbed
to its deadly thirst, and, crawling into a little volcanic bowl
to escape the cold winds of night, left their cuddled bones
there—where they were found many years later by Gov-

ernor Blaisdell and his surveyors, who gave Death Valley its
name. The valley lies in Inyo County, and is about one
hundred and fifty miles long. In width it tapers from three
miles at its southern end to thirty at the northern. It is
over two hundred feet below the sea-level. Most of Inyo
County is a great plateau, averaging 5000 feet in altitude;
and in it, in the south end of the Sierra Nevada range, towers the loftiest peak in the United States—Mount Whitney,
15,000 feet. So, as you may imagine, there is a terrible
"jumping-off-place" when one comes to the brink of this
accursed valley. From 5000 feet *above* sea-level to 200 feet
below it is a good deal of a drop; and in places it fairly looks
as if one might take it at a single jump. The valley is walled
on each side by savage and appalling cliffs which rise thousands of feet in apparently sheer walls. There are but few
places where the valley can well be crossed from side to side;
for by the time one has trudged over those miles of alkali
one is generally too far gone to climb up the farther rocks
to safety. It is the very last place. There is nothing so
deadly even in the hottest parts of Africa. Not even a bird
flies across that hideous waste—nature is absolutely lifeless
there. It is the dryest place in the world—the place where one
will soonest die of thirst, and where the victim soon becomes
a perfect mummy. When the melting snows of the Sierra
Nevada come roaring down the slopes in great torrents, they
do not reach the bottom of Death Valley. Long before the
stream can get there it is swallowed up into the thirsty air
and thirstier sands. The main party of pioneers crossed

Death Valley at about the middle, where it is but a few miles wide, but suffered frightfully there. With every day their tortures grew worse. The gaunt oxen were so nearly dead that their meat was rank poison; and at last the starving band had no food for four weeks save ox-hide scorched and then boiled to a bitter jelly. Day by day some of their number sank upon the burning sands, never to rise again. The skeleton survivors were too weak to help the fallen. One poor fellow named Isham revived enough to crawl four awful miles on his hands and knees in pursuit of his companions, and then died.

The strongest of the whole party was wee, nervous Mrs. Brier, who had come to Colorado an invalid, and who shared with her boys of four, seven, and nine years that indescribable tramp of nine hundred miles. For the last three weeks she had to lift her athletic husband from the ground every morning, and steady him a few moments before he could stand; and help wasted giants who a few months before could have held her upon their palms.

At last the few dying survivors crossed the range which shuts off that most dreadful of deserts from the garden of the world, and were tenderly nursed to health at the hacienda of a courtly Spaniard. Mr. Brier had wasted from one hundred and seventy-five pounds to seventy-five, and the others in proportion. When I saw him last he was a hale old man of seventy-five, cheerful and active, but with strange furrows in his face to tell of those by-gone sufferings. His heroic little wife was still living, and the boys, who had had a bitter ex-

perience such as perhaps no other boys ever survived, are
stalwart men.

The Great American Desert reaches from Idaho to the
Gulf of California and down into Mexico; and embraces
portions of Idaho, Wyoming, Utah, Nevada, Arizona, and
California. There have been numerous schemes to reclaim
parts of it—even to turning the Colorado River into its
southern basins—but all the ingenuity of man will never
change most of it from the irredeemable and fearful wilderness it is to-day.

IV

N and about the edges of the Great American Desert are many of the strangest corners. It seems as if Nature has crowded her curiosities into that strangest and most forbidding of museums, that they may not be too easily found.

A hundred miles north of the Petrified Forest, and well into the edge of the Arizona desert, are the seven strange and seldom visited Pueblo cities of Moqui. They all have wildly unpronounceable names: Hualpi, Si-chom-ivi, Shim-o-pavi, Shi-paui-luvi, Oraibe, and Mishongop-avi; and all are built on the summits of almost inaccessible mesas—islands of solid rock, whose generally perpendicular cliff-walls rise high from the surrounding plain. They are very remarkable towns in appearance, set upon dizzy sites, with quaint terraced houses of abode, and queer little corrals for the animals in nooks and angles of the cliff, and giving far outlook across the browns and yellows, and the spectral peaks of that weird plain. But they look not half so remarkable as they are. The most remote from civilization of all the Pueblos, the least affected by the Spanish influence which so wonder-

HUALPI — A MOQUI VILLAGE.

fully ruled over the enormous area of the southwest, and practically untouched by the later Saxon influence, the Indians of the Moqui towns retain almost entirely their wonderful customs of before the conquest. They number eighteen hundred souls. Their languages are different from those of any other of the Pueblos;* and their mode of life—though to a hasty glance the same—is in many ways unlike that of their brethren in New Mexico. They are the best weavers in America, except the once remarkable but now less skilful Navajos; and their *mantas* (the characteristic black woolen dresses of Pueblo women) and dancing-girdles are so famous that the Indians of the Rio Grande valley often travel three hundred miles or more, on foot or on deliberate burros, simply to trade for the long-wearing products of the rude, home-made looms of Moqui. The Moquis also make valuable and very curious fur blankets by twisting the skins of rabbits into ropes, and then sewing these together—a custom which Coronado found among them three hundred and fifty years ago, before there were any sheep to yield wool for such fabrics as they now weave, and when their only dress materials were skins and the cotton they raised.

It is in these strange, cliff-perched little cities of the Húpi ("the people of peace," as the Moquis call themselves) that one of the most astounding barbaric dances in the world is held; for it even yet exists. Africa has no savages whose

---

* Except that the one Moqui village of Tehua speaks the language of the Tehuas on the Rio Grande, whence its people came as refugees after the great Pueblo Rebellion of 1680.

mystic performances are more wonderful than the Moqui snake-dance—and as much may be said for many of the other secret rites of the Pueblos.

The snake is an object of great respect among all uncivilized peoples; and the deadlier his power, the deeper the reverence for him. The Pueblos often protect in their houses an esteemed and harmless serpent—about five or six feet long—as a mouse-trap; and these quiet mousers keep down the little pests much more effectively than a cat, for they can follow *shee-íd-deh* to the ultimate corner of his hole.

But while all snakes are to be treated well, the Pueblo holds the rattlesnake actually sacred. It is, except the *pichu-cuáte* (a real asp), the only venomous reptile in the southwest, and the only one dignified by a place among the "Trues." The *ch'ah-rah-ráh-deh* * is not really worshiped by the Pueblos, but they believe it one of the sacred animals which are useful to the Trues, and ascribe to it wonderful powers. Up to a generation ago it played in the marvelous and difficult superstitions of this people a much more important part than it does now; and every Pueblo town used to maintain a huge rattlesnake, which was kept in a sacred room, and with great solemnity fed once a year. My own pueblo of Isleta used to support a sacred rattler in the volcanic caves of the Cerro del Aire,† but it escaped five years ago, and the patient search of the officials failed to recover it. Very truthful old

* The Tee-wahn name is imitative, resembling the rattling. The Moquis call the rattlesnake *chú-ah*.

† Hill of the wind.

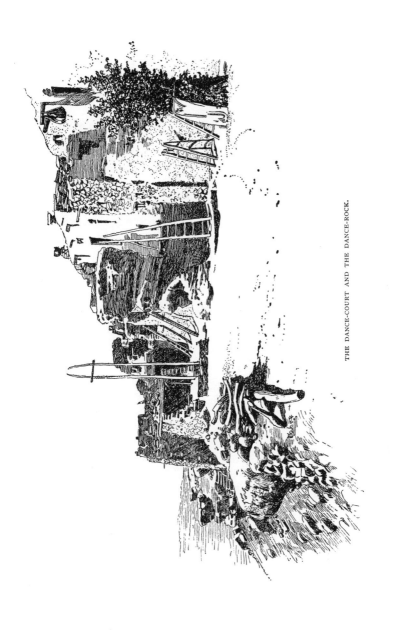

THE DANCE-COURT AND THE DANCE-ROCK.

men here have told me that it was nearly as large around as
my body; and I can believe it with just a *little* allowance, for
I myself have seen one here as large as the thickest part of
my leg.

There are many gruesome stories of human sacrifices to
these snakes, the commonest tale being that a baby was
chosen by lot from the pueblo once a year to be fed to *ch'ah-
rah-ráh-deh*. But this is of course a foolish fable. There are
no traces that the Pueblos ever practised human sacrifice in
any shape, even in prehistoric times; and the very grandfather of all the rattlesnakes could no more swallow the
smallest baby than he could fly.

This snake-tending has died out in nearly—and now, perhaps, in quite—all the New Mexican pueblos; but the curious trait still survives in the towns of Moqui. Every second
year, when the August moon reaches a certain stage (in 1891
it occurred on the 21st), the wonderful ceremony of the snake-
dance is performed; and the white men who have witnessed
these weird rites will never forget them.

For sixteen days beforehand the professional " Snake-men "
have been in solemn preparation for the great event, sitting in their sacred rooms, which are carved in the solid
rock. For many days before the dance (as before nearly
all such ceremonies with the Pueblos) no food must pass
their lips, and they can drink only a bitter " tea," called *máh-
que-be*, made from a secret herb which gives them security
against snake-poison. They also rub their bodies with prepared herbs.

Six days before the date of the dance the Snake-men go down the mesa into the plain and hunt eastward for rattle-snakes. Upon finding one, the hunter tickles the angry rep-tile with the "snake-whip"—a sacred bunch of eagle feathers —until it tries to run. Then he snatches it up and puts it into a bag. On the next day the hunt is to the north; the third day to the west; the fourth day to the south—which is, you must know, the only possible order in which a Pueblo dares to "box the compass." To start first south or north would be a dreadful impiety in his eyes. The captured snakes are then kept in the *kibva* (sacred room called "estufa" in the other pueblos), where they crawl about in dangerous freedom among the solemn deliberators. The night before the dance the snakes are all cleansed with great solemnity at an altar which the Snake-captain has made of colored sands drawn in a strange design.

The place where the dance is held is a small open court, with the three-story houses crowding it on the west, and the brink of the cliff bounding it on the east. Several sacred rooms, hollowed from the rock, are along this court, and the tall ladders which lead into them are visible in the picture. At the south end of the court stands the sacred Dance-rock —a natural pillar, about fourteen feet high, left by water-wearing upon the rock floor of the mesa's top. Midway from this to the north end of the court has been constructed the *keé-si*, or sacred booth of cotton-wood branches, its opening closed by a curtain. Just in front of this a shallow cavity has been dug, and then covered with a strong and ancient

5

plank with a hole in one side. This covered cavity represents *Shi-pa-pú*, the great Black Lake of Tears,—a name so
sacred that few Indians will speak it aloud,—whence, according to the common belief of all southwestern Indians, the
human race first came.

On the day of the dance the Captain of the Snake-men
places all the snakes in a large buckskin bag, and deposits
this in the booth. All the other active participants are still
in their room, going through their mysterious preparations.
Just before sunset is the invariable time for the dance.

Long before the hour, the housetops and the edges of the
court are lined with an expectant throng of spectators: the
earnest Moquis, a goodly representation of the Navajos, whose
reservation lies just east, and a few white men. At about
half-past five in the afternoon the twenty men of the Antelope Order emerge from their own special room in single file,
march thrice around the court, and go through certain sacred ceremonies in front of the booth. Here their captain
sprinkles them with a consecrated fluid from the tip of an
eagle feather. For a few moments they dance and shake
their *guajes* (ceremonial rattles made of gourds) in front of
the booth; and then they are ranged beside it, with their
backs against the wall of the houses. Among them are the
youngsters that day admitted to the order in which they will
thenceforward receive life-long training—dimpled tots of
from four to seven years old, who look extremely " cunning "
in their strange regimentals.

Now all is ready; and in a moment a buzz in the crowd

THE MOQUI INDIAN SNAKE-DANCE.

announces the coming of the seventeen priests of the Snake Order through the roofed alley just south of the Dance-rock. These seventeen enter the court in a single file at a rapid gait, and make the circuit of the court four times, stamping hard with the right foot upon the sacred plank that covers Shi-pa-pú as they pass in front of the booth. This is to let the *Cachinas* (spirits, or divinities) know that the dancers are now presenting their prayers.

When the captain of the Snake Order reaches the booth, on the fourth circuit, the procession halts. The captain kneels in front of the booth, thrusts his right arm behind the curtain, unties the sack, and in a moment draws out a big, squirming rattlesnake. This he holds with his teeth about six inches back of the ugly triangular head, and then he rises erect. The Captain of the Antelope Order steps forward and puts his left arm around the Snake-captain's neck, while with the snake-whip in his right hand he "smooths" the writhing reptile. The two start forward in the peculiar hippety-hop, hop, hippety-hop of all Pueblo dances; the next Snake-priest draws forth a snake from the booth, and is joined by the next Antelope-man as partner; and so on, until each of the Snake-men is dancing with a deadly snake in his mouth, and an Antelope-man accompanying him.

The dancers hop in pairs thus from the booth to the Dance-rock, thence north, and circle toward the booth again. When they reach a certain point, which completes about three-quarters of the circle, each Snake-man gives his head a sharp snap to the left, and thereby throws his snake to the

rock floor of the court, inside the ring of dancers, and dances
on to the booth again, to extract a fresh snake and make
another round.

There are three more Antelope-men than Snake-men, and
these three have no partners in the dance, but are intrusted
with the duty of gathering up the snakes thus set free and
putting them back into the booth. The snakes sometimes
run to the crowd—a ticklish affair for those jammed upon
the very brink of the precipice. In case they run, the three
official gatherers snatch them up without ado; but if they
coil and show fight, these Antelope-men tickle them with the
snake-whips until they uncoil and try to glide away, and then
seize them with the rapidity of lightning. Frequently these
gatherers have five or six snakes in their hands at once.
The reptiles are as deadly as ever—not one has had its
fangs extracted!

In the 1891 dance over one hundred snakes were used.
Of these about sixty-five were rattlesnakes. I stood within
six feet of the circle; and one man (a dancer) who came
close to me was bitten. The snake which he held in his
mouth suddenly turned and struck him upon the right cheek.
His Antelope companion *unhooked* the snake, which hung by
its recurving fangs, and threw it upon the ground; and the
pair continued the dance as if nothing had happened! Another man a little farther from me, but plainly seen, was bitten on the hand.

I never knew one of them to be seriously affected by a
rattlesnake's bite. They pay no attention to the (to others)

deadly stroke of that hideous mouth, which opens flat as a palm and smites exactly like one, but dance and sing in earnest unconcern. There is in existence one photograph which clearly shows the dancers with the snakes in their mouths—and only one. Beginning so late, and in the deep shadow of the tall houses, it is almost impossible for the dance to be photographed at all; but one year a lucky reflector of dense white cloud came up just before sunset and threw a light into that dark corner, and Mr. Wittick got the only perfect picture extant of the snake-dance. I have made pictures which do show the snakes; but they are not handsome pictures of the dance. The make-up of the dancers makes photography still harder. Their faces are painted black to the mouth, and white from that to the neck. Their bodies, naked to the waist, are painted a dark lake-red. They wear curious dancing-skirts to the knee, with beautiful fox-skins dangling behind, but nothing on their legs except rattles and sacred twigs at the ankle.

At last all rush together at the foot of the Dance-rock and throw all their snakes into a horrid heap of threatening heads and buzzing tails. I have seen that hillock of rattlesnakes a foot high and four feet across. For a moment the dancers leap about the writhing pile, while the sacred corn-meal is sprinkled. Then they thrust each an arm into that squirming mass, grasp a number of snakes, and go running at top speed to the four points of the compass. Reaching the bottom of the great mesa (Hualpi,* where the chief snake-dance

* Pronounced *Wól-pi.*

is held, is six hundred and sixty feet above the plain), they release the unharmed serpents.

These astounding rites last from half an hour to an hour, and end only when the hot sun has fallen behind the bald western desert. Then the dancers go to their sacred purification with the secret herb, and the awed on-lookers scatter to their quaint homes, rejoicing at the successful conclusion of the most important of all the public ceremonials of Moqui. It is believed by the Húpi that the rattlesnake was one of their first ancestors—the son of the Moqui Adam and Eve— and they have a very long and complicated folk-story about it. The snake-dance is therefore—among other superstitious aims—designed to please their divinities.

In the "neck" or "saddle" which connects the first of the Moqui "islands" of rock with the main table-land is a shrine of great importance. It is a little inclosure of slabs of stone surrounding a large stone fetich which has been carved into a conventional representation of the sacred snake. In two small natural cavities of the Dance-rock are also kept other large fetiches—both the latter being limestone concretions of peculiar shape.

This snake-dance seems to have been common to all the Pueblo towns in ancient times. Espejo saw it in Acoma in 1581; and there are to this day in other towns customs which seem to be survivals of this strange ceremony. In Isleta there are still men who have "power of snakes," and know how to charm them by putting the sacred corn-meal and corn-pollen on their heads — a practice which figures extensively in their folk-lore.

The Moquis make great numbers of remarkable-looking dolls for their children to play with; and in nearly every house some of these strange effigies are to be seen. They are toys for the youngsters, but not *merely* toys—they are also a sort of kindergarten course. They are called *cachinas*, and are supposed to represent the spirits in which the Moqueños believe. They are very clever representations of the outlandish figures of the masked men who take part in many ceremonial dances—these maskers, of course, being also supposed to look like the unseen but potent spirits. So a Moqui child very soon learns what the various spirits look like.

One of the oddities which a stranger will first notice in Moqui is the fashion in which the women dress their hair. The young girls have their abundant black locks done up in two large and very peculiar coils, one behind each ear. These coils stand far out from the head, like huge black buttons, and give a startling appearance to the wearer. Sometimes you would fancy that she has a pair of short, curving horns. But on close inspection one of these coils is found to resemble nothing else so much as a black squash-blossom in its full bloom—and that is exactly what it is designed to typify. Among the Húpi the squash-blossom is the emblem of maidenhood. Before marriage a girl must always wear her hair thus; but after marriage she must dress it in two pendent rolls, one by each ear. These rolls are supposed to resemble—and do resemble—the long, closed squash-blossom.

V.

T is interesting to notice that the Navajo Indians, who are the nearest neighbors of the Moquis, have superstitions widely different though quite as benighted. They will not touch a snake under any circumstances. So extreme are their prejudices that one of their skilled silversmiths was beaten nearly to death by his fellows for making to my order a silver bracelet which represented a rattlesnake; and the obnoxious emblem was promptly destroyed by the raiders— along with the offender's hut.

Living almost wholly upon game as they do, the Navajos cannot be prevailed upon to taste either fish or rabbit. I have known some very ludicrous things to happen when meanly mischievous Americans deluded Navajos into eating either of these forbidden dishes; and sometimes there have been very serious retaliations for the ill-mannered joke. Rabbits are wonderfully numerous in the Navajo country, being molested only by feathered and four-footed enemies; but the Indian who would fight to the death sooner than touch a delicious rabbit-stew is greedily fond of the fat and querulous prairie-dog. That whole region abounds in "dog-towns," and they are frequently besieged by their swarthy foes. A Navajo will stick a bit of mirror in the entrance of a burrow, and lie behind the little mound all day, if need be, to secure the coveted prize. When Mr. *Tusa* ventures from his bedroom, deep underground, he sees a familiar image mocking him at the front door; and when he hurries out to confront this impudent intruder, whiz! goes a chalcedony-tipped arrow through him, pinning him to the ground so that he cannot tumble back into his home, as he has a wonderful faculty for doing even in death; or a dark hand darts from behind like lightning, seizes his chunky neck safely beyond the reach of his chisel-shaped teeth, and breaks his spine with one swift snap.

But when the summer rains come, then is woe indeed to the populous communities of these ludicrous little rodents. As soon as the downpour begins, every adjacent Navajo between the ages of three and ninety repairs to the *tusa* village. They bring rude hoes, sharpened sticks, and knives, and every one who is able to dig at all falls to work, unmindful of the drenching. In a very short time a lot of little trenches are dug, so as to lead the storm-water to the mouths of as many burrows as possible; and soon a little stream is pouring down each.

"Mercy!" says Mr. *Tusa* to his fat wife and dozen chubby youngsters; "I wish we could elect aldermen that would attend to the drainage of this town! It's a shame to have our cellars flooded like this!"—and out he pops to see what can

be done. The only thing he can do is to swell the sad heap
of his fellow-citizens, over which strange two-footed babies,
far bigger than his, are shouting in wild glee. Such a rain-
hunt often nets the Navajos many hundred pounds of prairie-
dogs; and then there is feasting for many a day in the rude,
cold *hogans*, or huts of sticks and dirt which are the only
habitation of these Indians.

With the Pueblos, the mountain-lion or cougar is the king
of beasts—following our civilized idea very closely; but
with the Navajos the bear holds first rank. He is not only
the greatest, wisest, and most powerful of brutes, but even
surpasses man! The Navajo is a brave and skilled warrior,
and would not fear the bear for its deadly teeth and claws,
but of its supposed supernatural powers he is in mortal
dread. I have offered a Navajo shepherd, who had accident-
ally discovered a bear's cave, twenty dollars to show it to me,
or even to tell me in what cañon it lay; but he refused, in a
manner and with words which showed me that if I found the
cave I would be in danger from more than the bear. The
Indian was a very good friend of mine, too; but he was sure
that if he were even the indirect cause of any harm to the
bear, the bear would know it and kill him and all his family!
So even my princely offer was no inducement to a man who
was working hard for five dollars a month.

There is only one case in which the Navajos will meddle
with a bear. That is when he has killed a Navajo, and the
Indians know exactly which bear is the murderer. Then a
strong, armed party, headed by the proper religious officers

(medicine-men), proceed to the cave of the bear. Halting a short distance in front of the den, they go through a strange service of apology, which to us would seem entirely ludicrous, but to them is unutterably solemn. The praises of the bear, commander of beasts, are loudly sung, and his pardon is humbly invoked for the unpleasant deed to which they are now driven! Having duly apologized beforehand, they proceed as best they may to kill the bear, and then go home to fast and purify themselves. This aboriginal greeting, "I beg your pardon, and hope you will bear no resentment against me, but I have come to kill you," is quite as funny as the old farmer I used to know in New Hampshire, who was none too polite to his wife, but always addressed his oxen thus: "Now, if you please, whoa hish, Bary! Also Bonny! There! Thank you!"

The Navajos also make frequent prayers and sacrifices to the bear.

Under no circumstances will a Navajo touch even the skin of a bear. The equally dangerous mountain-lion he hunts eagerly, and its beautiful, tawny hide is his proudest trophy outside of war, and the costliest material for his quivers, bow-cases, and rifle-sheaths. Nor will he touch a coyote.

A Navajo will never enter a house in which death has been, and his wild domain is full of huts abandoned forever. Nor after he is married dare he ever see his wife's mother; and if by any evil chance he happens to catch a glimpse of her, it takes a vast amount of fasting and prayer before he feels secure from dangerous results. The grayest and most

6

dignified chief is not above walking backward, running like a scared boy, or hiding his head in his blanket, to avoid the dreaded sight.

Feathers figure very prominently in the religious customs of most aborigines, and remarkably so in the southwest. Among Navajos and Pueblos alike these plume-symbols are

PUEBLO PRAYER-STICKS.

of the utmost efficacy for good or bad. They are part of almost every ceremonial of the infinite superstitions of these tribes. Any white or bright-hued plume is of good omen — "good medicine," as the Indian would put it. The gay feathers of the parrot are particularly valuable, and some dances cannot be held without them, though the Indians have to travel hundreds of miles into Mexico to get them. A peacock is harder to keep in the vicinity of Indians than the finest horse — those brilliant plumes are too tempting.

Eagle feathers are of sovereign value; and in most of the pueblos great, dark, captive eagles are kept to furnish the coveted articles for most important occasions. If the bird of freedom were suddenly exterminated now, the whole Indian economy would come to a standstill. No witches could be exorcised, nor sickness cured, nor much of anything else accomplished.

Dark feathers, and those in particular of the owl, buzzard, woodpecker, and raven, are unspeakably accursed. No one will touch them except those who "have the evil road," — that is, are witches, — and any Indian found with them in his or her possession would be officially tried and officially put to death! Such feathers are used only in secret by those who wish to kill or harm an enemy, in whose path they are laid with wicked wishes that ill-fortune may follow.

How many of my young countrymen who have read of the "prayer-wheels" of Burmah, and the paper prayers of the Chinese, know that there is a mechanical prayer used by thousands of people in the United States? The Pueblo "prayer-stick" is quite as curious a device as those of the heathen Orient; and the feather is the chief part of it.

Prowling in sheltered ravines about any Pueblo town, the curiosity-seeker will find, stuck in the ground, carefully whittled sticks, each with a tuft of downy feathers (generally white) bound at the top.

Each of these sticks is a prayer — and none the less earnest and sincere because so misguided. Around the remote pueblo of Zuñi I have counted over three thousand of these strange invocations in one day's ramble; but never a tithe as many by any other pueblo.

According to the nature of the prayer, the stick, the feathers, and the manner of tying them vary. The Indian who has a favor to ask of the Trues prepares his feather-prayer with great solemnity and secrecy, takes it to a proper spot, prays to all Those Above, and plants the prayer-stick that it may continue his petition after he has gone home.

This use of the feather is also shared by the Navajos; and so is what may be called the smoke-prayer, in which the smoke of the sacred cigarette is blown east, north, west, south, up and down, to scare away the evil spirits and please the good ones.

In a corner of the Navajo country, too, is another curiosity of which few Americans are aware — a catacomb of genuine mummies! This is in the grim Cañon de Tsáy-ee,—ignorantly called "du Chelle,"—which is lined along the ledges of its dizzy cliffs with the prehistoric houses of the so-called Cliff-dwellers. These were not an unknown race at all, but our own Pueblo Indians of the old days when defense against savage neighbors was the first object in life.

These stone houses, clinging far up the gloomy precipice, were inaccessible enough at best, and are doubly so now that their ladders have crumbled to dust. In them are many strange relics of prehistoric times, and in some the embalmed bodies of their long-forgotten occupants. There is a still larger "deposit," so to speak, of American mummies in the wildly picturesque San Juan country, in the extreme north-western corner of New Mexico and adjacent parts of Colorado and Utah.   They are in similar cliff-built ruins, and belong to the same strange race.   So we have one of Egypt's famous wonders here at home.

The largest Indian tribes of the Colorado desert have from time immemorial cremated their dead on funeral pyres, after the fashion of the classic ancients and of modern India.   All the property of the deceased is burned in the same flames, and the mourners add their own treasures to the pile.   So prop-erty does not accumulate among the Mojaves, and there is no contesting of wills.

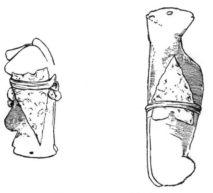

PUEBLO HUNTING FETICHES.

VI.

THE WITCHES' CORNER.

HIS very year at least one witch has been officially put to death in the United States, after an official trial. Last year many witches were executed, and many the year before, and many the year before that—and so on back for centuries. Is n't that a strange corner of our own country of which you did not dream? I shall never forget the awe which filled me when, soon after coming to New Mexico, I found myself in a land of active witchcraft. Of all the marvelous things in the unwritten southwest, the superstitions of the natives impressed me most deeply. I thought to have settled in New Mexico, U. S. A.; but it seemed that I had moved into another world and into the century before last. To hear my neighbors gravely discussing the condition of so-and-so, who "had been bewitched"; to have this and that person pointed out to me with the warning " *Cuidado de ella — es bruja!* "* to learn that an unfortunate was put to death yesterday "for being a witch"—it often made me pinch myself to see if I were not dreaming. But it was no dream.

* "Look out for her—she is a witch!"

The belief in witchcraft is a bitter reality in the wild southwest. There are some 175,000 souls in New Mexico, of
whom four fifths can neither read nor write, and about 30,-
000 of whom are Indians, 25,000 Americans, and the rest
Mexicans. Of course the Americans have no faith in
witches, nor do the educated Mexicans; but all the Indians
and probably ninety per cent. of the brave but ignorant
Mexicans are firm believers in this astounding superstition.
There are very few towns in this enormous territory most of
whose people do not believe in and dread one or more re-
puted witches among their own number; and in the Pueblo
towns and among the nomad Navajos and other Indians
witches are so numerous as to be the greatest of all dangers.
In my own pueblo of Isleta, which numbers over eleven hundred souls, nearly half the people are believed to be witches,
and the only thing which prevents a bloody war upon them
by the "True Believers" is fear of the Americans, of whom
there are several thousands only twelve miles away. It is
only a little while since a well-known young Indian of this
village was imprisoned and tortured (by the stocks and neck-
yoke) on formal accusation that he was a witch; and still less
time since my neighbor two doors away was executed at midnight, presumably for the same "crime"—since he was killed
in the specific manner prescribed by Tigua customs for the
slaying of witches. To keep down witchcraft is the foremost
official duty of the medicine-men; and when a witch is con-
victed, on accusation and "proof," it is the office of one of
the branches of medicine-men (the *kum-pah-whit-lah-wen,* or

guards) to execute him or her by shooting with an arrow through the whole body from left side to right side. Isleta is now one of the most civilized of the pueblos; its people are the kindest parents and the best neighbors I know; and yet the supernatural dread of supernatural harm turns them at times as far from their real selves as were our own god-fearing forefathers in New England when they burned poor old women alive. Sandia—a pueblo of the same tribe as Isleta (the Tiguas, or Tee-wahn)—a few leagues north of here, has been so decimated by the official killing-off of witches that it bids fair soon to become extinct; and these executions still continue. The first business of all "medicine-makings"—which are not to compound remedies for sickness alone, though that is "cured" by remarkable means, but to avert all dangers and invoke all prosperities for the town, its people, its animals, its crops, etc.—is to drive away and punish all witches who can be reached. So in all prayers, all dances, and in fact in all ceremonies whatever, the first service is to disperse the evil spirits who may be hovering about. When a child is born there are numerous ceremonials to keep it from being appropriated by the witches. When a person dies, the four days which his soul will take to reach the other world are filled by the medicine-men with the most laborious and astounding incantations and charms, with smoke to blind the eyes of the witches, and with false trails and other devices to throw them off the track of the journeying soul, lest they overtake it and swoop it away to the accursed land.

It needs very little to lay an Indian open to the suspicion

of having " the evil road." If he have red eyes, as though he had been awake o' nights, instead of sleeping peacefully as a good Indian should, he is at once looked upon with distrust. If he have an enemy, and that enemy becomes sick, it is still more convincing. The medicine-men will proceed secretly to search the house of the suspected person; and if they find any of the feathers of the accursed birds (the chief of which are the owl, raven, and woodpecker) or any other implements of witchcraft, his doom is sealed. To us it seems murder; but it is as judicial as our civilized punishments, for the sentence is pronounced by the recognized judges, and carried out by the official executioners. There are numerous charms against witches—quite as valuable as our own horseshoe over the door—and the boundless folk-lore of this strange people is full of the doings of " those of the evil road," and of the retribution with which they are always visited in the end.

Witchcraft is a common faith to all aborigines; so it is somewhat less surprising that the Pueblos believe in it, though they are so different from other Indians in so many important points.*   But my first encounter with witches and witch-believers was more astounding, for the people were actual citizens and voters of this enlightened republic !

Among the uneducated mass of Mexicans—who are the vast majority of their people here—the belief in *hechiseria* or *brujeria* (witchcraft) is as strong as among the Indians, though

---

* The Pueblos are, in fact, entitled to *all* the rights of American citizenship, including the ballot, under the solemn pledges our government made to Mexico in the treaty of Guadalupe Hidalgo, more than half a century ago; but they have never been given these rights.

their witches are less numerous. It is a remnant of the far
past. We have still the official records of many trials of
witches before Spanish courts in this territory, covering a
couple of centuries. Sometimes a whole bunch of witches
were tried at once, with all the solemnity of a high Spanish
tribunal, and those found guilty were duly put to death, just
as if they had been murderers.

Of later years the intelligence of the educated Mexicans
has rendered such trials no longer possible, and no Mexican
would think now of bringing a witch into court; but pro-
ceedings outside the law are not entirely done with. In
the year 1887, to my knowledge, a poor old Mexican woman
was beaten to death in a remote town by two men who believed they had been bewitched by her; and no attempt was
ever made to punish her slayers! A few months later I had
the remarkable privilege of photographing three "witches"
and some of the people they had "bewitched." One Mexican, of whom I have also a picture, claims that he was per-
manently crippled by these three poor women, and his right
leg *is* sadly twisted—though most of us would see in it more
of rheumatism than of witchcraft. But you never could make
Patapalo believe that. He had offended the women, and
afterward thoughtlessly drank some coffee they proffered;
and his leg at once grew crooked—what could be plainer
than that they had bewitched him?

A much more intelligent man than the poor town-butch-
er, Patapalo, tells—and believes—a much more astounding
story. He incurred the displeasure of a witch in San Mateo,

and is ready to make oath that she turned him into a woman ! He had to pay another witch in the distant cañon Juan de San Tafoya to turn him back to man again ! He is a person of whose sincere belief in this ridiculous statement there can be no doubt, and his intelligence in other matters emphasizes the depth of his superstitious ignorance in this. I know several other Mexicans who claim to have been bewitched in the same way; and the stories of minor misfortunes at the hands of the witches are innumerable. They can be heard in any New Mexican hamlet.

There is one good thing about Mexican witches—they never harm the dumb animals. Their sorceries are used only against human beings who have aroused their enmity. One who enjoys the rather dangerous reputation of being a witch is cordially feared and hated, but finds some compensations. Few Mexicans are reckless enough to refuse any gift or favor the supposed witch may ask. On the other hand, few dare eat anything offered by a witch, for in case they have un-wittingly offended her they are sure the food or drink will cause a live, gnawing animal to grow within them ! A favor-ite revenge of the witches is to make strange sores upon the face of the offender, which will not be healed until the witch is appeased by presents and draws out a stick or string or rag—somewhat after the fashion of the Pueblo wizards, of whom I will tell you presently. Other persons are made blind, or deaf, or lame. Indeed, almost any affliction which may befall one is very apt to be charged at once by these superstition-ridden people to some witch or other.

There are many very curious details in the Mexican witch-faith. No witch, for instance, can pass a sign of the cross; and a couple of pins or sticks placed in that shape effectually bars witches from entering the room or from emerging if the holy emblem is between them and the door. The spoken name of God or the Virgin Mary breaks a witch's spell at once. It is soberly related by many people of my acquaintance that they employed witches to bear them pick-a-back to great distances; but becoming alarmed at the enormous height to which the witches flew with them, they cried, "God save me!" or something of the sort, and instantly fell thousands of feet to the ground, but were not badly hurt!

Mexican witches do not fly about on broomsticks, like those in whom our forefathers believed, but in an even more remarkable fashion. By day they are plain, commonplace people, but at night they take the shapes of dogs, cats, rats, or other animals, and sally forth to witch-meetings in the mountains, or to prowl about the houses of those they dislike. So when the average Mexican sees a strange cat or dog about his home at night he feels a horror which seems out of place in a man who has proved his courage in bloody Indian wars and all the perils of the frontier.

When witches wish to fly, they generally retain their human form, but assume the legs and eyes of a coyote or other animal, leaving their own at home. Then saying (in Spanish, of course), "Without God and without the Virgin Mary," they rise into the air and sail away. A sad accident once befell a male witch named Juan Perea, whom I knew in San Mateo, but who died a couple of years ago. It was asserted that one night he went flying off with the eyes and legs of a cat, leaving his own on the kitchen table. His poor starved shepherd-dog overturned the table and ate the eyes, and Juan had to go through the rest of his life wearing the green eyes of a cat! That the pigmies of Africa should believe such things would not be strange; but what do you think of them as articles of faith for American voters?

You have all watched the "shooting stars" with wonder —but with no such feeling as that with which the natives here see them; for here those fiery hails are supposed to be witches, flying to their nightly meetings!

Any one bearing the blessed name of Juan (John) has the sole power of catching witches. All he has to do is to draw a nine-foot circle on the ground, turn his shirt inside out, and call the witch, who must at once fall helpless into this circle! As there are innumerable Juans here, they doubtless would have exterminated all the witches long ago, except for the unpleasant "fact" that whenever a John exercised this remarkable power all the other witches in the country fell upon him and beat him to death!

A drunken fellow in Cebolleta, a few years ago, kicked a witch. In revenge she caused a live mouse to grow in his stomach. The little rodent made its landlord's life miserable for a long time before he could bribe the witch to coax it out through his mouth!

These are fair samples of unnumbered thousands of stories which illustrate the firm faith of my neighbors in witchcraft.

7

It seems fairly childish to speak of them soberly, and yet they are implicitly believed by more citizens of the United States than there are in any New England city outside of Boston. In this strange corner of our country witchcraft is a concern of daily thought and dread, as it was in the older world a few centuries ago, when the same superstition splashed all Europe with the blood of unfortunate wretches. I have had even more intimate concern with witchcraft, both as accused and as victim. My photographic and other mysterious work has more than once led suspicious Indians to view me as a *hechicero;* and it is still the common belief among my aboriginal friends that I have been bewitched by some even more powerful wizard.

A stroke of paralysis in 1888 rendered my left arm powerless for more than three years and a half. The cause was simple enough—the breaking of a tiny blood-vessel in the brain. But my Indian friends—and even many Mexicans—smiled with a pitying superiority at this explanation. *They* would never swallow such a silly story—they knew well enough that I had been bewitched! Some even suggested that I should accuse the witch, and have him or her properly dealt with! My final complete recovery—thanks to a power- ful constitution and an out-door life—only confirmed their belief. Now they *knew* I had paid some other witch to cure me!

VII

OUR civilized "magicians," like Herrmann and his predecessors, earn their livelihood by exhibiting their marvelous dexterity, but without any claim to superhuman powers. They avowedly rely only upon their hands, educated to surpassing cleverness by tedious years of practice, and upon various ingenious machines and accessories. Perhaps this frankness, however, is partly due to the fact that any supernatural pretense would be laughed at by their intelligent auditors; and if we were all prepared to accept them as *real* magicians, I am not at all sure that they would not willingly pose as such.

With the aboriginal wizard there is no such stimulus to frankness. If his audiences have eyes incomparably less easy to be befooled than ours, their intellectual vision is less acute. To outdo even those matchlessly observant eyes, he

has only to be matchlessly adroit; and when the eyes are
once over-matched, his auditors are ready to accept any explanation he may choose to give.   He therefore claims supernatural powers, given to him by Those Above; and my
studies convince me that he himself believes this as fully as
do any of his people — so easy is it for us all, in time, to impose upon ourselves even more than upon others.

Superstition is the corner-stone of all the strange aboriginal religions.   Everything which the Indian does not absolutely understand he attributes to a supernatural cause —
and to a personified one.   The rainbow is a bow of the gods;
the lightning, their arrows; the thunder, their drum; the
sun, their shield.   The very animals are invested with supernatural attributes, according to their power to injure man or
to do him good.   In such a system as this a man who can
do or appear to do what others cannot is naturally regarded
as having superhuman gifts — in short, he is a wizard.   The
chief influence and authority with all aboriginal tribes lie in
their medicine-men, and these are always magicians.   They
have gained their ascendancy by their power to do wonderful and inexplicable things; and this ascendancy is main-
tained in the hands of a small, secret class, which never dies
out, since it is constantly recruited by the adoption of boys
into the order, to which their lives are thenceforth absolutely
devoted.   The life of a medicine-man is a fearfully hard one.
The manual practice alone which is necessary to acquire that
marvelous legerdemain is almost the task of a lifetime; and
there are countless enormous fasts and other self-denials,

which are so rigorous that these magicians seldom attain to the great age which is common among their people. With the Indian magicians as with ours, conjuring is the means of livelihood, but in a different and indirect way. They neither charge an admittance-fee nor take up a collection, but receive less direct returns from the faith of their fellow-aborigines that they are "precious to The Trues," and that their favor should be cultivated by presents. The jugglers of India, of whom we read so much, will exhibit their marvelous tricks to any one for a consideration; but no money in the world would tempt one of *our* Indian jugglers to admit a stranger to the place where he was performing his wonders. To him, as to his people, it is a matter not of money but of religion.

The aboriginal magicians with whom I am best acquainted are the medicine-men of the Navajo and Pueblo Indians of New Mexico, and astounding performers they are. It is impossible to say which are the more dextrous, though the Navajos have one trick which I have never seen equaled by the world's most famous prestidigitators. If these stern bronze conjurers had the civilized notion of making money by exhibiting themselves, they could amass fortunes. They have none of the cabinets, mirrors, false-bottomed cases, or other appliances of our stage-wizards; and they lack the greatest aid of the latter—the convenient sleeves and pockets. Their tricks are done in a bare room, with a hard clay floor under which are no springs or wires, with no accessories whatever.

The principal occasions of Pueblo and Navajo magic are

at the medicine-makings, when the people gather to see the
shamans (medicine-men) heal sickness, foretell the year, or
give thanks to The Trues for its prosperity, and perform
other rites belonging to such ceremonials.   These medicine-
makings among the Pueblos are held in one of the medicine-
houses — a great room sacred to the shamans and never to
be profaned by any other use.   There is one just behind the
Indian house in which I live.   The Navajos hold them in the
medicine-*hoganda* — a large conical hut, equally devoted to
this sole purpose.

After the preliminary prayers to Those Above, the disper-
sion of evil spirits, and other extremely curious and interesting ceremonies which I have no space to describe here,
the business of the medicine-dance is to cure those who are
sick or afflicted — that is, according to the Indian idea, bewitched.   There is no giving of remedies, as we understand
the phrase — all is magic.   The "medicine" (*wahr*, in the
language of this pueblo) is rather mental and moral than
physical;   and the doses are from nimble fingers and not
from vials.   An American "medicine-man" would open his
eyes very wide if he could see how these swarthy doctors put
up a prescription.

The shamans dance during the whole of their professional
duties, and most of the time have in each hand a long
feather from the wing of an eagle.   Earlier in the performance these feathers have been used to toss up evil spirits so
that the wind may bear them away;   but now they serve as
lancets, probes, and in fact the whole surgical-case and medi-

cine-chest. A shaman dances up to a sick person in the audience, puts the tip of the feather against the patient, and
with the quill in his mouth sucks diligently for a moment.
The feather seems to swell to a great size, as though some
large object were passing through it. Then it resumes its
natural size, the shaman begins to cough and choke, and
directly with his hand draws from his mouth a large rag, or
a big stone, or a foot-long branch of the myriad-bristling
buckhorn-cactus—while the patient feels vastly relieved at
having such an unpleasant lodger removed from his cheek or
neck or eye! No wonder he had felt sick! Sometimes the
magician does not use the feather at all, but with his bare
hand plucks from the body of the sick man the remarkable
"disease," which is waved aloft in triumph and then passed
around to the audience for critical inspection. In the whole
performance, it must be remembered, the wizards have not
even the advantage of distance, but are close enough to touch
the audience.

Common to these same medicine-dances is the startling
illusion of the witch-killing. In the bowl of sacred water
which stands before him, the chief shaman is supposed to see
as in a mirror everything that is happening in the whole
world, and even far into the future. At times, as he bends
to blow a delicate wreath of smoke from the sacred cigarette
across the magic mirror, he cries out that he sees witches in
a certain spot doing ill to some Indian. The *Cum-pah-huit-*
lah-wen (medicine-guards) rush out of the room with their
bows and arrows—which are the insignia of their office,

without which they must never appear—to get the witches. In a short time they return, bringing their victims by the long hair. These " dead witches" are in face, dress, and everything else exactly like Indians, except that they are no larger than a three-year-old child. Each has the feathers of an arrow projecting under the left arm, while the agate or volcanic glass tip shows under the right. Of course they are manikins of some sort; but the deception is sickeningly perfect. The guards swing them up to the very faces of the audience to be looked at; and sometimes drops of apparent blood spatter upon the awed spectators.

Another remarkable feat of these jugglers is to build upon the bare floor a hot fire of cedar-wood, so close as almost to roast the foremost of the audience. Then the dusky magicians, still keeping up their weird chant—which must never be stopped during the services—dance bare-footed and barelegged in and upon the fire, hold their naked arms in the flames, and eat living coals with smacking lips and the utmost seeming gusto. There can be no optical illusion about this —it is as plain as daylight. Of course there must have been some preparation for the fiery ordeal, but what it is no one knows save the initiated, and it is certainly made many hours beforehand, for the performers have been in plain sight for a very long time.

Another equally startling trick is performed when the room has been darkened by extinguishing the countless candles which gave abundant light on the other ceremonies. The awed audience sit awhile in the gloom in hushed ex-

"SUDDENLY A BLINDING FLASH OF FORKED LIGHTNING SHOOTS ACROSS THE ROOM."

pectancy. Then they hear the low growl of distant thunder, which keeps rolling nearer and nearer. Suddenly a blinding flash of forked lightning shoots across the room from side to side, and another and another, while the room trembles to the roar of the thunder, and the flashes show terrified women clinging to their husbands and brothers. Outside the sky may be twinkling with a million stars, but in that dark room a fearful storm seems to be raging. If one of these aboriginal Jupiters would condescend to superintend the lightnings for our theaters, we should have much more realistic stage-storms than we do. These artificial storms last but a few moments, and when they are over the room is lighted up again for the other ceremonies. How these effects are produced I am utterly unable to explain, but they are startlingly real.

The characteristic feature of one of the medicine-dances of the Beer-ahn here in Isleta is the swallowing of eighteen-inch swords to the very hilt, by the naked (except for the tiny breech-clout) performers. These swords are double-edged, sharp-pointed, and, as nearly as I can tell, about two inches wide. So far as I know, no other of the numerous classes of medicine-men here perform this feat.

In the great Navajo medicine-dance of Dsil-yíd-je Quacal, one of the most important ceremonies of the nine-days' "dance" is the swallowing of the "great plumed arrows" by the almost naked conjurers in similar fashion. After they have been withdrawn from the mouths of the magicians, the magical arrows (which have the ancient stone heads) are applied to the patient, being pressed to the soles of his feet, to his knees, hands, stomach, back, shoulders, crown of head, and mouth.

In this same remarkable and almost endless Navajo ceremonial, some of the magicians (generally in a band of ten or a dozen) perform the startling fire-dance. The conjurers are clad only in the breech-clout, and each carries in his hands a long bundle of shredded cedar-bark. The dance is performed around an enormous fire in a corral known as the Dark-Circle-of-Branches. Each lights his bark flambeau, and then they run at top speed around and around the bonfire. They hold their torches against their own nude bodies, then against those of their companions, often for two or three minutes at a time; they whip each other with these burning scourges, and rub each other down with them, taking and giving veritable baths of fire as they run madly around the circle, the flames streaming behind them in fiery banners. Dr. Washington Matthews, the foremost student of Navajo customs, has said officially: "I have seen many fire scenes on the stage, many acts of fire-eating and fire-handling by civilized jugglers, but nothing quite comparable to this."

Another Navajo jugglery is to stand a feather on end in a flaring, pan-shaped basket, and dance with it as a partner. The Indian—in this case sometimes the dancer is a very young boy—dances in proper fashion around the basket; and the feather dances too, hopping gently up and down, and swaying in the direction of its human partner. If he dances to the north, the feather leans northward; if he moves to the south, the feather tips southward, and so on, as if the quill were actually reaching out to him!

There is also "magic" in the foretelling of the year, which is done by the chief shaman and his two first-assistants. This medicine-dance is always by or before the middle of March, many weeks before a green blade of any sort is to be found in this climate. These three officials go out from the meeting to the banks of the Rio Grande, and presently return with stalks of green corn and wheat—which they declare was brought to them by the river direct from The Trues. These stalks are handed about among the audience, and then the chief shaman draws from them the omens for the crops of the coming season.

The last service of the medicine-dance before the benediction-song is the "seed-giving," which is itself a sleight-of-hand trick. The chief fetich of the shamans is "the Mother"— an ear of spotless white corn with a plume of downy white feathers bound to the head. It represents the mother of all mankind, and during the whole medicine-dance one of these queer objects has been sitting in front of each medicine-man. Now, as all in the audience rise, the chief shaman and his assistants shake their "Mothers" above the heads of the throng in token of blessing; and out pours a perfect shower of kernels of corn, wheat, and seeds of all kinds, in a vastly greater quantity than I would undertake to hide in ten times as many of those little tufts.

The most remarkable of the feats of the Pueblo magicians is one of which I cannot write in detail, for I have never

8

seen it; but that the trick is performed, and so well done as to deceive the sharpest-eyed of the spectators, is a fact beyond doubt. The shamans are said at some special occasions to turn themselves at will into any animal shape; and where a moment before had stood a painted Indian the audience sees a wolf, or bear, or dog, or some other brute! This is in a line with some of the most famous juggleries of India, and is quite as wonderful a deception as any of them.

These are by no means the only tricks in the repertory of the Pueblo conjurers, but they are sufficient to illustrate the marvelous dexterity and adroitness of these swarthy wonder-workers, who produce such surprising results with none of the paraphernalia of more civilized jugglers, and whose magic has such a deep interest beyond its mere bewilderment of the eye. It is one of the potent factors in a religion so astonishing and so vastly complicated that whole volumes would hardly exhaust the interest of the subject.

The Navajo magicians practise all these tricks and numerous others. One of their manifestations which I have never found among the Pueblos is the "moving of the sun." This takes place in the medicine-lodge at night—the time of *all* official acts of the medicine-men. At the appointed time a sun rises on the east (inside the room) and slowly describes an arched course until at last it sets in the west side of the room, and darkness reigns again. During the whole performance a sacred chant is kept up, and once started dare not be interrupted until the sun has finished its course.

But the crowning achievement of the Navajo—and, in my

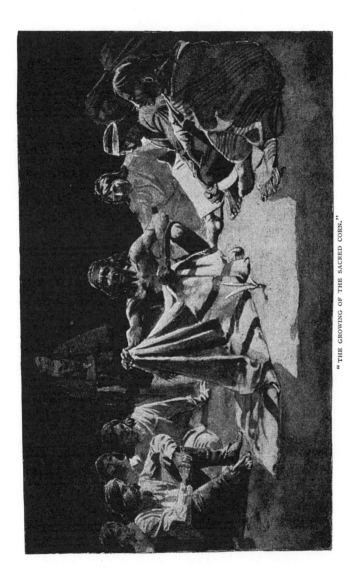

"THE GROWING OF THE SACRED CORN."

knowledge, of any Indian—magicians is the growing of the sacred corn. At sunrise the shaman plants the enchanted kernel before him, in full view of his audience, and sits solemnly in his place singing a weird song. Presently the earth cracks, and the tender green shoot pushes forth. As the magician sings on the young plant grows visibly, reaching upward several inches an hour, waxing thick and putting out its drooping blades. If the juggler stops his song the growth of the corn stops, and is resumed only when he recommences his chant. By noon the corn is tall and vigorous and already tasseled-out; and by sunset it is a mature and perfect plant, with its tall stalk, sedgy leaves, and silk-topped ears of corn! How the trick is performed I have never been able to form so much as a satisfactory guess; but done it is, as plainly as eyes ever saw anything done, and apparently with as little chance for deception.

VIII.

THE SELF-CRUCIFIERS.

ROM the witches, and within the same strange corner of our country where they still flourish, it is an easy step to a much more wonderful fanaticism, to the most wonderful, perhaps, in the limits of the civilized world. It is a relic of a barbarism so incredible that one can hardly blame those who could not believe it possible. I should have been as skeptical myself, though thousands of Americans have seen it, if I had not myself viewed the astounding sight. And in corroboration of my eyes there are beside me a score of photographs, which very nearly cost me my life in the taking, and several times since.

You may have learned that in the Middle Ages nearly the whole of Europe had a strange epidemic—a fever of penitential self-whipping. The Flagellants, as they were called, paraded the streets lashing themselves with scourges, or used the whip at home. Even kings caught the infection, and abused their own royal backs. It took centuries to eradicate this remarkable custom. There is nothing left of it in Europe now; and one who wishes to see so strange a sight must go not abroad but to a neglected corner of our own land.

When I read in boyhood of the awful self-tortures of the Fakeers of India, I little dreamed that I should come to live among a class of men who fully parallel their worst self-cruelties, and men who are citizens of the United States, with votes as good as mine.

The Penitentes or Penitent Brothers were once very numerous in New Mexico, but have been quietly stamped out by the Church until but few active bands remain, and they only in the most out-of-the-way hamlets. They are Mexicans, and of course very ignorant and fanatic ones. Their strange brotherhood—a remnant and perversion of the penitent orders of the Middle Ages—is active only forty days in the year, the forty days of Lent. At that time they flog their own naked backs with cruel scourges of aloe-fiber, carry enormous crosses, lie on beds of cactus, and perform similar self-tortures, making pilgrimages thus. On Good Friday they redouble their ghastly efforts, and finally crucify, upon a real cross, one of their number who is chosen by lot. He does not always die under this awful torture, but when he does, nothing is done to his fanatical brethren.

I shall never forget my first encounter with the Penitentes at San Mateo, N. M., in 1888, and there are very good reasons why I should not. Among them is a ball in my throat. If the discovery that I was living among witches had startled and aroused me, you may imagine my feelings when, some months later, I learned that a living man was to be crucified in town in a few days. This was learning something about my own country with a vengeance. The first hint came one belated night as I returned from hunting in the mountains. Suddenly there rose upon the air the most awful sound I ever heard. The hideous scream of the mountain-lion, the deadly war-whoop, are tame beside it. You may laugh at me for being scared at the simple whistle of a reed, but if ever you hear that unearthly ululation you will shiver too. Words cannot describe its piercing, wild, uncanny shrill. The official *pitero* afterward taught me that simple air, and it sounds very flat indeed when whistled; but blown from his shrieking reed, filling the air for miles so that one cannot tell whether it comes from above, below, or either hand, it is as ill a sound as you will ever wish to hear.

When I got home to my courtly Spanish friends and asked the meaning of that unearthly *too-ootle-tee-oo* they told me about the Penitentes. It was Monday of Holy Week, and they were making their nightly pilgrimages; on Thursday and Friday I could see them. What, in daylight? Oh, yes. Hurrah! Then I will photograph them! *Por dios amigo,* but they will kill you if you think of such a foolhardy thing! But who ever knew an enthusiast to be a coward in the line of his hobby? If I had been certain of being killed the next moment, it is not sure that I should not have tried to get the photographs first, so wrought up was I. And make the photographs I did, twenty-five of them, with my one useful hand quaking on the bulb of the Prosch shutter and now and then snapping an instantaneous picture at the marvelous sight, with a cocked six-shooter lying on the top of the camera-box, and lion-like Don Ireneo and a stalwart peon with revolvers in hand facing back the murderous mob. Perhaps the pictures were not worth the risk of that day and of the many subsequent months when repeated attempts were made to assassinate me; but they are the only photographs that were ever made of that strangest of the strange corners of our country, and I have never grudged the price. I afterward got photographs of several of the chief Penitentes; and have in my cabinet some of their blood-stained scourges, procured at equal risk.

That was in 1888. The same year there were, to my knowledge, crucifixions in two other New Mexican towns, and whipping and the other rites in twenty-three. In 1889, 1890, and 1891 there were again crucifixions in San Mateo and one other town that I know of, and there may have been more. Until within four years there were also women-Penitentes, but so far as I can learn they are no longer active. They used to wind all their limbs with wire or ropes so tightly as to stop the circulation, bear crosses, and march for miles with unstockinged feet in shoes half filled with sharp pebbles.

And these are your fellow-citizens and mine! What do you think about going to Africa to find barbarous customs, or to Oberammergau for a Passion-play?

IX

HOMES THAT WERE FORTS.

N Indian who dwells in a house at all seems an anomaly to most of us, who know none too much of our own country. We picture him always as a nomad, living in his wigwam or tepee of bark or hide for a few days at a time, and then moving his "town" elsewhere. The astounded look of the average traveler when he learns that we have Indians who build and inhabit permanent and good dwellings of many stories in height is never to be forgotten.

There are some tribes of recently civilized aborigines in the Indian Territory who have learned to dwell in fairly good farm-houses within a generation, and other remnants of tribes elsewhere; but these all learned the habit from us, and recently. There is but one Indian tribe in North America above Mexico which has always lived in permanent houses since history began, and that is one of our very largest tribes, the Pueblos. When Columbus was yet trying to beat a New World into the thick skull of the Old, these simple, unlettered "village Indians" were already living in their strange but comfortable and lofty tenements, and no man knows for how long before. And in very similar houses they dwell to-day, and in very much the same style as before the first European eyes ever saw America. It took a great many generations for our forefathers to attain to any buildings of more than fifty rooms and three stories in this New World; but unknown centuries before the landing of the Pilgrims — or even of the Spaniards, who were more than a hundred years ahead of them — the ignorant Indians of the southwest built and occupied huge houses from four to six stories in height, and with sometimes half a thousand rooms.* The influence of civilization has largely affected Pueblo architecture; and most of the Indian towns along the Rio Grande nowadays have but one- and two-storied structures, more after the Spanish style. But there are hundreds of ruins of these enormous "community-houses" scattered over the two territories of Arizona and New Mexico, and some in Colorado and Utah, and some still occupied towns of the same sort The most striking example among living towns is the pueblo of Taos,† in the extreme northern part of New Mexico. That wonderfully picturesque town, looking at which the traveler finds it hard to realize that he is still in America, has but two houses; but they are five and six stories high, and contain about three hundred rooms apiece. The pueblo of Acoma, in a western county, has six houses, each three stories tall, and Zuñi, still farther

---

* Pecos had two houses of five hundred and seventeen and five hundred and eighty-five rooms respectively.

† Reached by a twenty-five-mile-wagon-ride from Embudo, on the Denver and Rio Grande Railway.

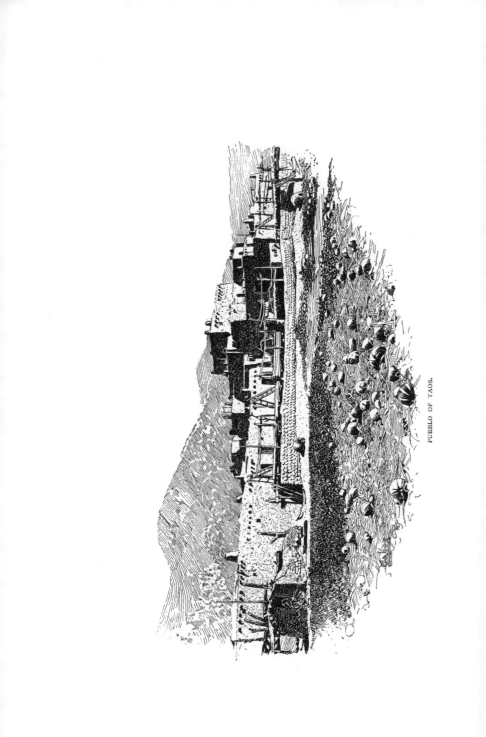

PUEBLO OF TAOS.

west, has a six-story community-house covering many acres and containing many hundred rooms. The Moqui towns are three-storied. As for ruins of such buildings, they are everywhere. Some years ago I found in a remote and dangerous corner of the Navajo country such a ruin—the type of a thousand others—in which the five-story community-house formed an entire rectangle, inclosing a public square in the middle. The outer walls of these houses never had doors or windows, so they presented to any marauding foe a blank wall of great height. On one side of this ruin is its most uncommon feature—a great tower, with part of the fifth story still standing, and still showing the loopholes by which the beleaguered Pueblos showered agate-tipped arrows upon their besiegers. This pueblo was a deserted and forgotten ruin when the first Spaniards entered this territory, three hundred and fifty years ago.

All these great houses were of stone masonry very well laid. The builders had no metal of any sort, and therefore could not dress stone, as many superficial observers have supposed they did, but selected sandstones and limestones which broke naturally into rather regular shape, and laid these in mud mortar with remarkable skill. Down the uncrumbled masonry of those prehistoric walls one can slide the point of a spade as down a dressed plank.

The architecture of the Pueblos is unique and characteristic, and their original houses look unlike anything else in the world. They are all *terraced*, so that the front of a building looks like a gigantic flight of steps. The second

9

story stands well back on the roof of the first, which thus gives it a sort of broad, uncovered porch its whole length. The third story is similarly placed upon the second, and so on up. There are no stairs inside even the largest of these buildings, except sometimes ladders to go down into the first story when that is built in the old fashion without doors. In Acoma, which has about seven hundred people, there were, when I first knew it, but six doors on the ground, and there are but few more now. To get into the first story of any of the hundreds of other tenements, one must go up a ladder to the first roof, enter the second-story room, lift a wee trap-door in its floor, and back down another ladder to the first-floor room. All the "stairs" are outside the house, and can be moved from place to place—a plan which has its advantages as well as its drawbacks—for they are all simply tall, clumsy ladders.

All these architectural peculiarities were for purposes of defense. The lower story was a dead wall, into which no enemy with only aboriginal weapons could break, and some of these walls have laughed at civilized field-pieces. The ladders could easily be drawn up, and the level roofs made an excellent position from which to rain stones and arrows upon a foe. Even if the enemy captured the first roof, the people had only to retire to the second, from which they could fight down with undiminished advantage. From these terraces the inhabitants could hold their own against a far superior force. Besides, the tenements were generally built around a square, so that their sheer back walls presented a cliff-like and

AN ANCIENT CLIFF-DWELLING.

unbroken obstacle which no savage foe could scale, while
their fronts faced upon the safe inner inclosure. At Pecos
(now deserted), which was the largest pueblo in the southwest,
and at many smaller towns, an Indian could step from his
door and walk around the whole town on any one of the tiers
of roofs.   Sometimes these community-houses were terraced
on both sides; and the two at Taos are like huge pyramids,
terraced on all four sides.

These fine stone walls were generally plastered inside and
out with adobe clay, which made them very smooth and neat,
particularly when brilliantly whitewashed, according to the
Pueblo custom, with gypsum.   The rafters are the straight
trunks of tapering pines stripped of their bark, and above
these is a roof of cross-sticks, straw, and clay, which is
perfectly water-tight.   The windows are all small—another
relic of the old days of danger—and in the more primitive
houses the windows are only translucent sheets of gypsum.
Nearly every room has its queer southwestern fireplace, in
which the sticks are burned on end.   Those for heating alone
are very tiny, and stand in a corner; but the cooking fireplaces often fill one side of a room, and under one of their
capacious "hoods" nearly a dozen people could sit.

As you may imagine from what has been said of their
houses, the Pueblos are very peculiar and interesting Indians
They live very neatly and comfortably, and their homes are
generally as clean as wax.   They are peaceable and industrious, good hunters and brave warriors when need be, but
quiet farmers by profession, as they were when the outside

PART OF CAÑON DE TSÁY-EE.

world first found them.   They have always elected their own
offitials, and they obey the laws both of their own strange
government and of the United States in a way which they
certainly did not learn from us, for there is *no* American
community nearly so law-abiding.   They are entirely self-
supporting, and receive nothing from our government.   They
are not poor nor lazy, and they do not impose servile tasks
upon their wives.   One of my Pueblo neighbors in Isleta lent
the hard cash to pay off our troops in New Mexico during
the civil war!

Quite as interesting and remarkable as the best types of
present Pueblo communal houses are the ruins of their
still more ancient homes.   It was long supposed that the
so-called "Cliff-builders" and "Cave-dwellers" were of an
extinct race; and much more of silly and ignorant surmise
than of common-sense truth has been written about them.
But as soon as there was any really scientific investigation
of the southwest, like Bandelier's wonderful researches, the
fact was fully and finally established that the builders of
these great ruins were nothing in the world but Pueblo
Indians.   They have not "vanished," but simply moved, for
a variety of reasons; and their descendants are living to
this day in later pueblos.   Indeed, we now know the history
of many of these ruins; and the Indians themselves, that of
all or nearly all.

The Pueblos used always to build in places which Nature
herself had made secure, and generally upon the top of *mesas*,
or "islands" of rock.   Those who settled among the peculiar

terraced cañons which abound in some parts of the southwest usually built their towns upon the shelves of the cliff;
while those whose region furnished precipices of easily carved
stone hollowed out caves therein for their dwellings.   It all
depended on the locality and the surroundings.

A cañon of the "Cliff-builders" is a wonderfully picturesque and interesting place.   The stratification was a great
help to the builders of these strange chasm-towns, and doubtless first suggested to them the idea of putting their houses
there.   The cliffs are many times as far apart, in such a
cañon, at their tops as at the bottom, and a cross-section of
the cañon would look something like this:

Sometimes there is a perennial stream at the bottom, but
oftener, in this arid region, the dry season leaves only a chain
of pools, which were, however, adequate for the water-supply
of these communities.   The several lower shelves of the
gorge were never built upon, and the water was all carried
several hundred feet up the cliff in earthen jars or tight-
woven baskets on the heads of the industrious housewives.
Such inconvenience of the water-works has never deterred
the Pueblos, and it is a striking commentary upon the savage dangers of their old life to see at what a fearful expense

of toil they brought water any distance to a place that was *safe*. At Acoma to this day every drop of drinking-water is brought in jars half a mile over an enormously difficult cliff trail, and in some of the old-time pueblos the daily water-journey was even worse. They never brought water thus and filled tanks inside the town, as some have fancied, but stored it only in their earthen *tinajas*.

But safety was before water, and so the swarthy people built their homes far up the side of the cliff, and *there* was a great saving of labor in another way. As a rule the alternate strata in those cañons are of different kinds of rock, and unequally eroded. Between each pair of harder strata the softer intermediate one had been so gnawed out by wind

CLIFF-VILLAGE ON THE MANCOS.

A NIGHT ATTACK OF APACHES UPON THE CLIFF-FORTRESS.

and water that its neighbors above and below projected many feet beyond it, the lower one always farthest; so there the "Cliff-builder" found that nature had made ready to his hand three of the six sides of every room. The smooth, solid rock of the shelf was his floor, and a narrow but endless porch outside as well. The overhanging rock of the ledge above was his roof—frequently a very low one, but certainly water-tight—and the face of the intermediate stratum was his back wall. He had only to build three little stone walls from stone floor to stone roof—a front wall and two end walls—and there was his house.

These cliff-rooms were extremely small, varying according to the strata, but seldom more than a dozen feet long, eight or ten feet deep, and five to eight feet high. In many of them no ordinary person could stand erect. There were seldom any windows; and the doors, which served also as chimneys, were very low and but twelve to eighteen inches wide. An enemy at the very door would be so crouched and cramped in entering, that those within could take him at a disadvantage.

Think of a town whose sidewalks were three or four feet wide, and more than that number of hundred feet apart, and between them a stupendous gutter five hundred feet deep! Think of those fat, dimpled, naked brown babies, whose three-foot play-ground had no fence against a tumble of half a thousand feet!

There are several of these cañons of the "Cliff-builders" easily accessible from the A. & P. R. R. at Flagstaff, Arizona.

They are gigantic gashes in the level uplands; one comes to their very brink without the remotest suspicion that such an abyss is in front. One of these cañons is over twenty miles long, and in places six hundred feet deep. It contains the ruins of about a thousand of these small cliff-houses, some of which are very well preserved. These are the easiest to reach of any of this class of ruins, being less than ten miles from the railroad station and hotels. There are hundreds of other cañons in Arizona, New Mexico, and the lower corners of Colorado and Utah presenting the same sort of cliff-houses; but most of them are in the wilderness, at great distances from the railroad or any other convenience of civilization.

In most of these houses there is little to be found. Furniture they never had, and most of the implements have been carried away by the removing inhabitants or by subsequent roving Indians. The floors are one and two feet deep with the dust of ages, mingled with nut-shells and thorns brought in by the rock-squirrels which are now the only tenants. Digging is made painful by a thousand thorn-stabs and by stifling clouds of that flour-like dust; but it is often rewarded. All about are strewn broken bits of prehistoric pottery, and the veriest mummies of corn-cobs, shrunken by centuries of that dry air to the size of a finger and hardened almost to flint. There are also occasional squash-stems, as wizened and as indurated. By digging to the bed-rock floor I have found fine stone axes, beautiful agate arrow-points, the puzzling discoidal stones, and even baskets of yucca fiber exactly like the strange "plaques" made in Moqui to-day. The baskets

RUINED CAVE-VILLAGE, CAÑON DE TSÁY-EE.

10

crumbled to dust soon after they were exposed to the air. There are few other countries so dry that a basket of slender vegetable threads would hold its patterns for four hundred years or more under a foot of soil.

Between the small cliff-houses already described and the cave-dwellings there is a very curious link—houses, or even whole towns, built in a natural cave. "Montezuma's Castle" is such a one, and there are many, many others, of which probably the best-known—thanks to Jackson's expedition— are the fine ruins on the Mancos. Most of the important ruins of the Cañon de Tsáy-ee and its tributaries, Cañon del Muerto and Monumental Cañon, are also of this class. These caves are not, like the Mammoth Cave, great subter- ranean passages, but great hollows, generally like a huge bowl set up on edge in the face of the cliff. They absolutely protect the inclosed town (which is frequently one building of enormous size) above, on both sides, and generally also below. They are usually high up from the bottom of the cliff, and between them and the foot is a precipitous ascent which no enemy could scale if any resistance whatever were made. Such towns could be captured only by surprise, as we know that in very rare cases some were captured. Some observant but uninformed travelers have been sadly misled by the regular, round cavities which are found in the ground near these lofty pueblos, and have taken them for water-tanks. Such a notion could arise only from entire ignorance both of the history and the ethnology of the south- west. These circular cavities are the remains of the estufas,

THE CUEVA PINTADA, OR "PAINTED CAVE."

or sacred rooms of the men, which were generally made underground. The roofs have long ago disappeared, and only these pits are left. They never had anything more to do with water than the fireplaces had; the Pueblo reservoirs were something entirely different.

These huge houses were generally far from regular, for the simple reason that there never was a "master-architect" to control the structure. Every family built its part of the tenement to suit itself. There could be no "bossing" in such things, for Indians are essentially tribal, and under that organization anything like a feudal authority is an absolute impossibility. Still, the builders agreed fairly well as to the general plan, and the great structure was sometimes very symmetrical.

The romantic Cueva Pintada,* which not a dozen white men have ever seen, is a very good type of these caves on a smaller scale, being only some fifty feet in diameter. It looks very much like the bowl of a gigantic ladle set into the cliff fifty feet above its foot. It contains several cave-dwellings, but no houses of masonry, though these occur at other points of the cliff.

To me the real cave-dwellings are the most interesting of all these strange sorts of prehistoric ruins. They are probably no older than the cliff-built houses; as I have said, those differences were not of time, or development, or tribe, but merely of locality, but they *seem* so much farther from us.

---

* "Painted Cave," so called from the strange pictographs in red ocher which adorn its concave walls.

To see them carries one back to the times when our own
ancestors and all mankind dwelt in caves and wore only the
skins of wild beasts; those far, dim days when there was not
even iron, nor any other metal, and when fire itself was new,
and the savage stomach was all the conscience and all the
brains that man knew he had.

The most extensive and wonderful cave-communities in
the world are in the great Cochití upland, some fifty miles
northwest of Santa Fé.   The journey is a very laborious one,
but by no means dangerous; and if you can get my good
Indian *compadre** José Hilario Montoya, now governor of
the pueblo of Cochití, to guide you, you are apt to remember
it as the most interesting expedition of your life.   The country itself is well worth a long journey to see, for it is one
of the wildest in North America.   The enormous plateau is
split with cañons from the mountains to the deep-worn river;
and the *mesas* which separate them are long triangles which
break off in thousand-foot cliffs in the chasm of the Rio
Grande, their narrow points looking like stupendous columns, whence they get their Spanish name *potreros*.   The
whole area is like the foot of some unspeakable giant with
dozens of toes, set down beside the hoarse, gray river.

The whole region for thousands of square miles—like the
majority, indeed, of New Mexico—is volcanic.   But here we
see less of the vast lava-flows so common in other parts of
the territory.   Instead, there is an unprecedented deposit of
further-consumed matter from the forgotten fire-mountains.

* Chum.

MUMMY CAVE AND VILLAGE, CAÑON DEL MUERTO, ARIZONA.

When I was a boy in New England, I thought the "*floating stone*" with which I scrubbed my dingy fists was a great curiosity; but in the gorges of the Cochití upland are cliffs one thousand five hundred feet high, and miles long, of solid pumice. *There* is enough "stone that will float" to take the stains from all the boy hands in the world for all time.

In this noble and awesome wilderness several tribes of Pueblo Indians dwelt in prehistoric times. It probably did not take them long to learn that in such a country of soft cliff it was rather easier to dig one's house than to build it, even when the carpenter had no better tools than a sharp splinter of volcanic glass. The volcanoes did some good, you see, in this land which they burned dry forever; for in the same cliff they put the soft stone from which any one could cut a house, and nuggets of the extremely hard glass which the same eruption had made, wherefrom to chip the prehistoric "knife."

In the superbly picturesque cañon of the Rito de los Frigoles* is the largest of all villages of caves, deserted for more than four hundred years. Outside its unnumbered cave-rooms were more rooms yet, of masonry of "bricks" cut from the same cliff.

A few miles farther up the Rio Grande, not down in a cañon but on the top of the great plateau nearly two thousand feet above the river, are two huge castle-like buttes of chalky tufa, each some two hundred feet high. They stand one on each side of the dividing gulf of the Santa Clara cañon, and are

* "Brook of the beans."

known to the Indians respectively as the Pu-yé and the Shú-fin-ne. They are the most easily accessible of the large cave-villages of North America, being not over ten miles from the little railroad town of Española, on the Rio Grande some thirty miles by rail from Santa Fé. Going up the lovely Santa Clara cañon, past the now inhabited pueblo of that name, along the musical trout-brook to where an old mill once stood among the tall pines, one can clamber up a trail on either side of the cañon to the plateau at the top, and thence less than an hour's walk will take one to either of these great aboriginal honeycomb homes. The Pu-yé, which is on the south side of the cañon, is the largest, and has many hundreds of cave-rooms. They are burrowed out everywhere in the foot of the perpendicular white cliff, in tiers one above the other to a height of three stories. The caves are small, generally round rooms eight to twelve feet in diameter, with arched ceilings and barely high enough to allow a man to stand upright. The old smooth plaster on the walls remains to this day, and so do the little portholes of windows, and the niches for trinkets. In some places there is even a second cave-room back of the first. Here, and at the Rito, the estufas were carved out of the cliff, like the other rooms, but larger. Upon the top of the cliff, and in an almost impregnable position, are the ruins of a large square pueblo built of blocks of tufa—evidently the fortress and retreat of the dwellers in the caves in case of a very desperate attack. Against any ordinary assault, the masonry houses "down-stairs," so to speak, with their inner cave-rooms, were safe

THE WHITE HOUSE, CAÑON DE TSÁY-EE.

enough.   These houses of masonry at the foot of the cliff
have all fallen; but in the rocks the mortises which held the
ends of their rafters are still plainly visible.

In this same wild region are the only great stone idols (or,
to speak more properly, fetiches) in the United States—the
mountain lions of Cochití.   They are life-size, and carved from
the solid bed-rock on the top of two huge mesas.   To this
day, the Indians of Cochití before a hunt go to one of these
almost inaccessible spots, anoint the great stone heads, and
dance by night a wild dance which no white man has seen or
ever will see.

11

X.

FAR southwest of Moqui, and still in the edge of the great Dry Land, is what I am inclined to rank as the most remarkable area of its kind in the southwest—though in this wonderland it is difficult enough to award that preëminence to any one locality. At least in its combination of archæologic interest with scenic beauty and with some peerless natural curiosities, what may be called the Mogollon watershed is one of the most startling regions in America or in the world.

The Mogollones* are not a mountain system as Eastern people understand the phrase. There is no great range, as among the Appalachians and the Rockies. The "system" is merely an enormous plateau, full three hundred miles across, and of an average height above the sea greater than that of any peak in the East: an apparently boundless plain, dotted only here and there with its few lonely "hangers-on" or "parasites" of peaks,—like the noble San Francisco triad

* Spanish, "The hangers-on."

near Flagstaff,—which in that vast expanse seem scarce to
attain to the dignity of mounds. On the north this huge
table-land melts into hazy slopes; but all along its southern
edge it breaks off by sudden and fearful cliffs into a country
of indescribable wildness. This great territory to the south,
an empire in size, but largely desert and almost entirely wilderness, has nevertheless the largest number of considerable
streams of any equal area in the thirsty southwest. The
Gila, the Rio Salado,* the Rio Verde, and others—though
they would be petty in the East, and though they are small
beside the Rio Grande and the Colorado—form, with their
tributaries, a more extensive water-system than is to be found
elsewhere in our arid lands. The Tonto† Basin—scene of
one of the brave Crook's most brilliant campaigns against
the Apaches—is part of this wilderness. Though called a
"basin," there is nothing bowl-like in its appearance, even
as one sees down thousands of feet into it from the commanding "Rim" of the Mogollones. It is rather a vast chaos
of crags and peaks apparently rolled into it from the great
breaking-off place—the wreck left by forgotten waters of
what was once part of the Mogollon plateau.

About this Tonto Basin, which is some fifty miles across,
cluster many of the least-known yet greatest wonders of our
country. South are the noble ruins of Casa Grande, and all
the Gila Valley's precious relics of the prehistoric. The Salt
River Valley is one of the richest of fields for archæologic

* "Salt River," a fine stream whose waters are really salt at points
where great springs well up.
† "Tonto" is Spanish for fool.

research; and the country of the Verde is nowise behind it. All across that strange area of forbidding wildernesses, threaded with small valleys that are green with the outposts of civilization, are strewn the gray monuments of a civilization that had worn out antiquity, and had perished and been forgotten before ever a Caucasian foot had touched the New World. The heirlooms of an unknown past are everywhere. No man has ever counted the crumbling ruins of all those strange little stone cities whose history and whose very names have gone from off the face of the earth as if they had never been. Along every stream, near every spring, on lofty lookout-crags, and in the faces of savage cliffs, are the long-deserted homes of that mysterious race—mysterious even now that we know their descendants. Thousands of these homes are perfect yet, thousands no more changed from the far, dim days when their swart dwellers lived and loved and suffered and toiled there, than by the gathered dust of ages. Very, very few Americans have ever at all explored this Last Place in the World. It has not been a score of years known to our civilization. There is hardly ever a traveler to those remote recesses; and of the Americans who are settling the pretty oases, a large proportion have never seen the wonders within a few leagues of them. It is a far, toilsome land to reach, and yet there is no reason why any young American of average health should not visit this wonderland, which is as much more thrilling than any popular American resort as the White Mountains are more thrilling than Coney Island on a quiet day.

The way to reach this strangely fascinating region is by the Atlantic and Pacific Railroad to Prescott Junction, Arizona, four hundred and twenty-eight miles west of Albuquerque. Thence a little railroad covers the seventy miles to Prescott; and from Prescott one goes by the mail-buckboard or by private conveyance to Camp Verde, forty-three miles. Camp Verde is the best headquarters for any who would explore the marvelous country about it. Comfortable accommodations are there; and there can be procured the needful horses — for thenceforward horseback travel is far preferable, even when not absolutely necessary. There is no danger whatever nowadays. The few settlers are intelligent, law-abiding people, among whom the traveler fares very comfortably.

The Verde* Valley is itself full of interest; and so are all its half-valley, half-cañon tributaries — Oak Creek, Beaver Creek, Clear Creek, Fossil Creek, and the rest. Away to the north, over the purple rim-rock of the Mogollones, peer the white peaks of the San Francisco range (one can also come to the Verde from Flagstaff, by a rough but interesting eighty-mile ride overland). All about the valley are *mesas*,† and cliffs so tall, so strange in form and color, so rent by shadowy cañons as to seem fairly unearthly. And follow whatever cañon or cliff you will, you shall find everywhere more of these strange ruins. They are so many hundreds,

---

* Rio Verde, "Green River," — so called from the verdure of its valley, which is in such contrast with its weird surroundings.

† Table-lands.

MONTEZUMA'S WELL.

that while all are of deep interest I can here describe only the more striking types.

Beaver Creek enters the Rio Verde about a mile above the now abandoned fort. Its cañon is by no means a large one, though it has some fine points. A long and rocky twelve miles up Beaver, past smiling little farms of to-day that have usurped the very soil of fields whose tilling had been forgotten when history was new, brings one to a wonder which is not "the greatest of its kind," but the *only*. There is, I believe, nothing else like it in the world.

It has been named—by the class which has pitted the southwest with misnomers—"Montezuma's Well." It is hardly a well,—though an exact term is difficult to find,—and Montezuma* never had anything to do with it; but it is none the less wonderful under its misfit name. There is a legend (of late invention) that Montezuma, after being conquered by Cortez, threw his incalculable treasure into this safest of hiding-places; but that is all a myth, since Montezuma had no treasures, and in any event could hardly have brought the fabled tons of gold across two thousand miles of desert to this "well," even if he had ever stirred outside the pueblo of Mexico after the Spaniards came—as he never did. But as one looks into the awesome abyss, it is almost easy to forget history and believe anything.

At this point, Beaver Creek has 'eaten away the side of a rounded hill of stone which rises more than one hundred feet above it, and now washes the foot of a sheer cliff of striking picturesqueness. I can half imagine the feelings of the first white man who ever climbed that hill. Its outer show gives no greater promise of interest than do ten thousand other elevations in the southwest; but as one reaches a flat shoulder of the hill, one gets a first glimpse of a dark rift in the floor-like rock, and in a moment more stands upon the brink

---

* The war-chief of an ancient league of Mexican Indians, and *not* "Emperor of Mexico," as ill-informed historians assert.

of an absolutely new experience. There is a vast, sheer well, apparently as circular as that peculiar rock could be broken by design, with sides of cliffs, and with a gloomy, mysterious lake at the bottom. The diameter of this basin approximates two hundred yards; and its depth from brink of cliff to surface of water is some eighty feet. One does not realize the distance across until a powerful thrower tries to hurl a pebble to the farther wall. I believe that no one has succeeded in throwing past the middle of the lake. At first sight one invariably takes this remarkable cavity to be the crater of an extinct volcano, like that in the Zuñi plains already referred to; but a study of the unburnt limestone makes one give up that theory. The well is a huge "sink" of the horizontal strata in one particular undermined spot, the loosened circle of rock dropping forever from sight into a terrible subterranean abyss which was doubtless hollowed out by the action of springs far down in the lime-rock. As to the depth of that gruesome, black lake, there is not yet knowledge. I am assured that a sounding-line has been sent down three hundred and eighty feet, in a vain attempt to find bottom; and that is easily credible. Toss a large stone into that midnight mirror, and for an hour the bubbles will struggle shivering up from its unknown depths.

The waters do not lave the foot of a perpendicular cliff all around the sides of that fantastic well. The unfathomed "slump" is in the center, and is separated from the visible walls by a narrow, submerged rim. One can wade out a few feet in knee-deep water,—if one have the courage in that "creepy" place,—and then, suddenly, as walking from a parapet, step off into the bottomless. Between this water-covered rim and the foot of the cliff is, in most places, a wild jumble of enormous square blocks, fallen successively from the precipices and lodged here before they could tumble into the lower depths.

There are two places where the cliff can be descended from top to water's edge. Elsewhere it is inaccessible. Its dark, stained face, split by peculiar cleavage into the semblance of giant walls, frowns down upon its frowning image in that dark mirror. The whole scene is one of utter grimness. Even the eternal blue of an Arizona sky, even the rare fleecy clouds, seem mocked and changed in that deep reflection.

Walking around the fissured brink of the well eastward, we become suddenly aware of a new interest—the presence of a human Past. Next the creek, the side of the well is nearly gone. Only a narrow, high wall of rock, perhaps one hundred feet through at the base, less than a score at the top, remains to keep the well a well. On one side of this thin rim gapes the abyss of the well; on the other the abyss to the creek. Upon this wall—leaving scarce room to step between them and the brink of the well, and precariously cling-ing down the steep slope to the edge of the cliff that over-hangs the creek—are the tousled ruins of a strong stone building of many rooms, the typical fort-home of the ancient Pueblos. Its walls are still, in places, six to eight feet high; and the student clearly makes out that the building was of two and three stories. It was a perfect defense to the Indians who erected it; and was not only safe itself on that commanding perch, but protected the approach to the well. This is the only town I know of that was ever builded upon a natural bridge; as some houses in this same region are probably the only ones placed *under* such a. curiosity.

Leading from the center of this fort-house, the only easy trail descends into the well; and *it* is so steep that no foe could prosper on it in the face of any opposition. This brings us to a tiny green bench six or eight feet above the level of the dark lake, where two young sycamores and a few live-oak bushes guard a black cavity in the overhanging cliff. We look across the dark waters to the western wall, and are startled to see in its face a perfect cliff-house, perched where the eagle might build his nest. A strange eerie for a home, surely! There, on a dizzy little shelf, overhung by a huge flat rock which roofs it, stands this two-roomed type of the human dwelling in the old danger-days. From its window-hole a babe might lean out until he saw his dimpled image in the somber sheet below. Only at one end of the house, where a difficult trail comes up, is there room on the shelf for a dozen men to stand. In front, and at its north end, a goat could scarce find footing. The roof and floor and rear wall are of the solid cliff, the other three walls of stone masonry, perfect and unbroken still. A few rods along the face of the rock to the north is another cliff-dwelling not so large nor so well preserved; and farther yet is another. It is fairly appalling to look at those dizzy nests and remember that they were *homes!* What eagle-race was this whose warriors strung their bows, and whose women wove their neat cotton tunics, and whose naked babes rolled and laughed in such wild lookouts—the scowling cliff above, the deadly lake so far below! Or, rather, what grim times were those when farmers *had* to dwell thus to escape the cruel obsidian knife* and war-club of the merciless wandering savage!

But if we turn to the sycamore at our back, there is yet more of human interest. Behind the gray debris of the cliff gapes the low-arched mouth of a broad cave. It is a weird place to enter, under tons that threaten to fall at a breath; but there have been others here before us. As the eye grows wonted to the gloom, it makes out a flat surface beyond. There, forty feet back from the mouth, a strong stone wall stretches across the cave; and about in its center is one of the tiny doors that were characteristic of the southwest when a doorway big enough to let in a whole Apache at a time was unsafe. So the fort-house balanced on the cliff-rim between two abysses and the houses nestled in crannies of the bald precipice were not enough—they must build far in the very caves! That wall shuts off a large, low, dark room. Beyond is another, darker and safer, and so on. To our left is another wall in the front of another branch of the cave; and in that wall is a little token from the dead past. When I went there in June, 1891, my flash-light failed, and I lit a dry *entraña†* to explore during the hour it would take the lens

* The only knives in those days were sharp-edged flakes of obsidian (volcanic glass) and other stone.
† The buckhorn-cactus, which was the prehistoric candle.

to study out part of the cave in that gloom. And suddenly
the unaccustomed tears came in my eyes; for on the flinty
mortar of that strange wall was a print made when that
mortar was fresh adobe mud, at least five hundred years
ago, maybe several thousands,—the perfect imprint of a
baby's chubby hand. And of that child, whose mud autograph has lasted perhaps as long as Cæsar's fame, who may
have wrought as deep impression on the history of his race
as Cæsar on the world's, we know no more than that careless
hand-print, nor ever shall know.

This left-hand cave is particularly full of interest, and is
probably the best remaining example of this class of home-
making by the so-called "Cliff-dwellers." With its numerous
windings and branches, it is hundreds of feet in length; and
its rooms, formed by cross-walls of masonry, extend far into
the heart of the hill, and directly under the fort-house. It
seems to have been fitted for the last retreat of the people in
case the fortress and the cliff-houses were captured by an
enemy. It was well stored with corn, whose mummied cobs
are still there; and—equally important—it had abundant
water. The well *seems* to have no outlet—the only token of
one visible from within being a little rift in the water-mosses
just in front of the caves. But in fact there is a mysterious
channel far down under the cliff, whereby the waters of the
lake escape to the creek. In exploring the main cave one
hears the sound of running water, and presently finds a place
where one may dip a drink through a hole in the limestone
floor of a subterranean room. The course of this lonely little

brook can be traced for some distance through the cave, below whose floor it runs. Here and there in the rooms are lava hand-mills and battered stone hammers, and other relics of the forgotten people.

Returning to the creek at the foot of the hill, and following the outer cliff up-stream a few hundred feet, we come to a very picturesque spot under a fine little precipice whose foot is guarded by stately sycamores. Here is the outlet of the subterranean stream from the well. From a little hole in the very base of the cliff the glad rivulet rolls out into the light of day, and tumbles heels over head down a little ledge to a pretty pool of the creek.

The water of the well is always warmish, and in winter a little cloud of vapor hovers over the outlet. Between the cliff and the creek is pinched an irrigating-ditch, which carries the waters of the well half a mile south to irrigate the ranch of a small farmer. Probably no other man waters his garden from so strange a source.

12

XI.

MONTEZUMA'S CASTLE.

OMEWHAT more than half-way back from Montezuma's Well to Camp Verde, but off the winding road, is another curiosity, only less important, known as "Montezuma's Castle." It is the best remaining specimen of what we may call the cave-pueblo—that is, a Pueblo Indian "community-house" and fortress, built in a natural cave. The oft-pictured ruins in the Mancos cañon are insignificant beside it.

Here the tiny valley of Beaver Creek is very attractive. The long slope from the south bank lets us look far up toward the black rim of the Mogollones, and across the smiling Verde Valley to the fine range beyond. On the north bank towers a noble limestone cliff, two hundred feet high, beautifully white and beautifully eroded. In its perpendicular front, half-way up, is a huge, circular natural cavity, very much like a giant basin tilted on edge; and therein stands the noble pile of "Montezuma's Castle." A castle it truly looks, as you may see from the illustration—and a much finer ruin than many that people rush abroad to see, along

"MONTEZUMA'S CASTLE," SEEN FROM BEAVER CREEK.

the historic Rhine. The form of the successive limestone
ledges upon which it is built led the aboriginal builders to
give it a shape unique among its kind.

It is one of the most pretentious of the Pueblo ruins, as it
is the most imposing, though there are many hundreds that
are larger.

From the clear, still stream, hemmed in by giant sycamores
that have doubtless grown only since that strange, gray ruin
was deserted, the foot of the cliff is some three hundred feet
away. The lowest foundation of the castle is over eighty feet
above the creek; and from corner-stone to crest the building
towers fifty feet. It is five stories tall, over sixty feet front
in its widest part, and built in the form of a crescent. It
contains twenty-five rooms of masonry; and there are, besides, many cave-chambers below and at each side of it—
small natural grottos neatly walled in front and with wee
doors The timbers of the castle are still in excellent preservation,—a durability impossible to wood in any other climate,—and some still bear the clear marks of the stone axes
with which they were cut. The rafter-ends outside the walls
were "trimmed" by burning them off close. The roofs and
floors of reed thatch and adobe mud are still perfect except
in two or three rooms; and traces of the last hearth-fire that
cooked the last meal, dim centuries ago, are still there. Indeed, there are even a few relics of the meal itself—corn,
dried cactus-pulp, and the like.

The fifth story is nowhere visible from below, since it
stands far back upon the roof of the fourth and under the

hanging rock. In front it has a spacious veranda, formed by the roof of the fourth story, and protected by a parapet which the picture shows with its central gateway to which a ladder once gave access. It is only the upper story which can be reached by an outside ladder—all the others were accessible only through tiny hatchways in the roofs of those below. So deep is the great uptilted bowl in which the castle stands, so overhanging the wild brow of cliff above, that the sun has never shone upon the two topmost stories.

There is but one way to get to the castle, and that is by the horizontal ledges below. These rise one above the other (like a series of shelves, *not* like steps), ten to fourteen feet apart, and fairly overhang. The aborigines had first to build strong ladders, and lay them from ledge to ledge; and then up that dizzy footing they carried upon their backs the uncounted tons of stones and mortar and timbers to build that great edifice. What do you imagine an American architect would say, if called upon to plan for a stone mansion in such a place? The original ladders have long ago disappeared; and so have the modern ones once put there by a scientist at the fort. I had to climb to the castle by a crazy little frame of sycamore branches, dragging it after me from ledge to ledge, and sometimes lashing it to knobs of rock to keep it from tumbling backward down the cliff. It was a very ticklish ascent, and gave full understanding how able were the builders, and how secure they were when they had retreated to this high-perched fortress and pulled up their ladders—as they undoubtedly did every night. A monkey

"MONTEZUMA'S CASTLE," FROM THE FOOT OF THE CLIFF.

could not scale the rock; and the cliff perfectly protects the castle above and on each side. Nothing short of modern weapons could possibly affect this lofty citadel.

Down in the valley at its feet—as below Montezuma's Well and the hundreds of other prehistoric dwellings in the cañon of Beaver—are still traces of the little fields and of the *acequias* * that watered them. Even in those far days the Pueblos were patient, industrious, home-loving farmers, but harassed eternally by wily and merciless savages—a fact which we have to thank for the noblest monuments in our new-old land.

* The characteristic irrigating-ditches of the southwest.

XII.

OU all know of the Natural Bridge in Virginia, and perhaps have heard how the first and greatest president of the United States, in the athletic vigor of his youth, climbed and carved his name high on its cliff. A very handsome and picturesque spot it is, too; but if a score of it were thrown together side by side, they would not begin to make one of the Natural Bridge of which I am going to tell you—one in the western edge of the Tonto Basin, Arizona, in the same general region as Montezuma's Well and Castle, but even less known than they.

The Natural Bridge of Pine Creek, Arizona, is to the world's natural bridges what the Grand Cañon of the Colorado is to the world's chasms—the greatest, the grandest, the most bewildering. It is truly entitled to rank with the great natural wonders of the earth—as its baby brother in Virginia is not. Its grandeur is equally indescribable by artist and by writer —its vastness, and the peculiarities of its "architecture," make it one of the most difficult objects at which camera was ever leveled. No photograph can give more than a hint of its appalling majesty, no combination of photographs more than hints. There are photographs which do approximate justice to bits of the Grand Cañon, the Yosemite, the Yellowstone, the Redwoods, Niagara*; there never will be of the Natural Bridge of Arizona—for reasons which you will understand later. But perhaps with words and pictures I can say enough to lead you some time to see for yourself this marvelous spot.

From Camp Verde the Natural Bridge lies a long, hard day's ride to the southeast. There is a government road—a very good one for that rough country—to Pine, so one may go by wagon all but five miles of the way. This road is fifteen miles longer to Pine than the rough and indistinct mail-trail of thirty-eight miles, which a stranger should not attempt to follow without a guide, and a weak traveler should not think of at all. About midway, this trail crosses the tremendous gorge of Fossil Creek—down and up pitches that try the best legs and lungs—and here is a very interesting spot. In the north side of Fossil Creek Cañon, close to the trail and in plain sight from it, are lonely little cave-houses that look down the sheer cliffs to the still pools below. Several miles down-stream there is a fort-house, also. Where the trail crosses the cañon there is no running water except in the rainy season; but a few hundred yards further down are the great springs. Like hundreds of other springs in the west, they are so impregnated with mineral that they are

---

* Whose majestic Indian name, *Nee-ah-gáh-rah,* is quite lost in our flat corruption *Nigh-ágg-ara.*

constantly building great round basins for themselves, and for a long distance flow down over bowl after bowl. But unlike other springs, those of Fossil Creek build their basins of what seems crude Mexican onyx. The fact that these waters quickly coat twigs or other articles with layers of this beautiful mineral gives rise to the name of Fossil—almost as odd a misnomer as has the "Petrified Spring" of which a New Mexico lady talks.

Passing through lonely Strawberry Valley, with its log farm-houses among prehistoric ruins, one comes presently over the last divide into the extreme western edge of the Tonto Basin, and down a steep cañon to the stiff little Mormon settlement of Pine, on the dry creek of the same name. From there to the Natural Bridge—five miles down-stream —there is no road at all, and the trail is very rough. But its reward waits at the end. Leaving the creek altogether and taking to the hills, we wind among the giant pines, then across a wild, lava-strewn mesa, and suddenly come upon the brink of a striking cañon fifteen hundred feet deep. Its west wall is an unspeakably savage jumble of red granite crags; the east side a wooded, but in most places impassably steep bluff. The creek has split through the ruddy granite to our right a wild, narrow portal, below which widens an almost circular little valley, half a mile across. Below this the cañon pinches again, and winds away by grim gorges to where the blue Mazatzals bar the horizon.

In the wee oasis at our feet there is as yet no sign of a natural bridge, nor of any other colossal wonder. There is

LOOKING THROUGH THE SOUTH ARCH OF THE GREATEST NATURAL BRIDGE.

13

a clearing amid the dense chaparral—a clearing with tiny house and barn, and rows of fruit trees, and fields of corn and alfalfa. They are thirteen hundred feet below us. Clambering down the steep and sinuous trail, among the chapparo and the huge flowering columns of the maguey, we come quite out of breath to the little cottage It is a lovely spot, bowered in vines and flowers, with pretty walks and arbors by which ripples the clear brook from a big spring at the very door. A straight, thick-chested man, with twinkling eyes and long gray hair, is making sham battle with a big rooster, while a cat blinks at them from the bunk on the porch. These are the only inhabitants of this enchanted valley—old "Dave" Gowan, the hermit, and his two mateless pets. A quaint, sincere, large-hearted old man is he who has wrought this little paradise from utter wilderness by force of the ax. Only those who have had it to do can faintly conceive the fearful toil of clearing off these semi-tropic jungles. But the result gives the hermit just pride. His homestead of one hundred and sixty acres contains a farmlet which is not only as pretty as may be found, but unique in the whole world.

It is well to have this capable guide, for there is nowhere an equal area wherein a guide is more necessary. Think of Gowan himself, familiar for years with his strange farm, being lost for three days within a hundred yards of his house. That sounds strange, but it is true.

The old Scotchman is very taciturn at first, like all who have really learned the lessons of out-of-doors, but promptly

accedes to a request to be shown his bridge. He leads the
way out under his little bower of clematis, down the terraced
vineyard, along the corn-field, and into the pretty young orchard of peach and apricot. Still no token of what we seek;
and we begin to wonder if a bridge so easily hidden can be
so very big after all. There is even no sign of a stream.

And on a sudden, between the very trees, we stand over a
little water-worn hole and peer down into space. *We are on
the bridge now! The orchard is on the bridge!* Do you know
of any other fruit-trees that grow in so strange a garden?
Of any other two-storied farm? The rock of the bridge is
at this one point less than ten feet thick; and this odd little
two-foot peep-hole, like a broken plank in the giant floor,
was cut through by water.

"Wait," chuckles the hermit, his eyes twinkling at our
wonder; "wait!" And he leads us a few rods onward, till
we stand beside an old juniper on the very brink of a terrific
gorge. We are upon the South Arch of the bridge, dizzily
above the clear, noisy stream, looking down the savage cañon
in whose wilds its silver thread is straightway lost to view.
The "floor" of the bridge here, as we shall also find it at the
North Arch, has broken back and back toward its center, so
that a bird's-eye view shows at each side of the bridge a horizontal arch. A ground plan of the valley would look something like the sketch on the opposite page.

Circling south along the southeast "pier," we start down a
rugged, difficult, and at times dangerous trail. A projecting
crag of the pier — destined to be a great obstacle, later, in

our photographic attempts—shuts the bridge from view till
we near the bottom of the gorge, and then it bursts upon us
in sudden wonder.   The hand of man never reared such an
arch, nor ever shall rear, as the patient springs have gnawed
here from eternal rock.   Dark and stern, and fairly crushing

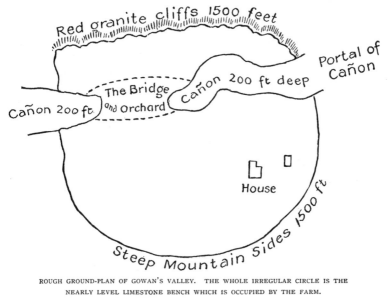

ROUGH GROUND-PLAN OF GOWAN'S VALLEY.   THE WHOLE IRREGULAR CIRCLE IS THE
NEARLY LEVEL LIMESTONE BENCH WHICH IS OCCUPIED BY THE FARM.

in its immensity, towers that terrific arch of rounded limestone.   The gorge is wild beyond telling, choked with giant
boulders and somber evergreens and bristling cacti until it
comes to the very jaws of that grim gateway, and there even
vegetation seems to shrink back in awe.   Now one begins to

appreciate the magnitude of the bridge, a part of whose top holds a five-acre orchard. In its eternal shadow is room for an army.

The South Arch, to which we have thus come, is the larger and in some respects the more imposing. From its top to the surface of the water is two hundred feet, and the pools are very deep. The span of the archway is over two hundred feet as we see it now from without; but we shall soon find it to be really very much greater. The groined limestone is smoothly rounded; and the fanciful waters seem to have had architectural training—for the roof is wonderfully rounded into three stupendous domes, each flanked by noble flying buttresses of startling symmetry. A photograph of that three-domed roof would be a treasure; but it is among the many impossibilities of this baffling place.

Climbing up the water-worn bed-rock into the cool dusk of the bridge—for the sun has never seen one-tenth of the way through this vast tunnel—we stand under the first dome. Away up to our left, on the west side of the stream, there is a shelf at the top of an impressive wall; and mounting by ledges and a tall ladder, we find this little shelf to be an enormous level floor, running back three hundred feet west. Here, then, we see the extreme span of the bridge, over five hundred feet; and here we find the central pier—a stupendous column from this floor to the vaulted roof, a column more than one hundred feet in circumference. How strange that the blind waters which ate out all the rest of this vast chamber should have left that one necessary pillar to support the roof!

ANOTHER VIEW OF THE GREAT BRIDGE.

About midway of the stream's course under the bridge is the Great Basin — a pool which would be a wonder anywhere. It is a solid rock bowl, some seventy-five feet in diameter and ninety in depth; and so transparent that a white stone rolled down the strange natural trough over one hundred feet long in the side of the basin can be seen in all its bubbling course to the far bottom of that chilly pool. Fifty of the beautiful "Basin" in the Franconia Notch would not make one of this; and the noble "Pool" itself, in the same mountain paradise, does not match it. The clear stream pours into this basin in a white fall of thirty feet; but, dwarfed by its giant company, the fall seems petty.

The North Arch — to which we may come under the bridge by a ticklish climb around the Great Basin — is less regular but not less picturesque than the South Arch. It is more rugged in contour, and its buttresses, instead of being smooth, are wrought in fantastic figures, while strange stalactites fringe its top and sides.

And now for the comparative magnitude of this greatest of natural bridges. Its actual span is over five hundred feet — that is, about five times the span of the Virginia Bridge. Its height from floor of bridge to surface of water is forty feet less than its small brother's; but to the bottom of erosion — the proper measurement, of course — it is fifty feet greater. But in its breadth — that is, measurement up and down stream — it is over *six hundred feet*, or more than twelve times as wide as the Virginia Bridge! So you see one could carve, from this almost unknown wonder, something like *sixty* bridges, each equal to the greatest curiosity of Virginia!

In these vast proportions lies the impossibility of adequately photographing this bridge.   There is no point from which the eye can take it in at once. It is a wonder-book which must be turned leaf by leaf.   Miles of walking are necessary before one really understands.   From the bed of the stream half the dignity of the arch is lost behind the boulders, if one gets off far enough to command the opening at a glance.   If near enough for an unobstructed view, then the vast arch so overshadows us that neither eye nor lens can grasp it all. And the wing-cliff which projects from the southeast pier— as you may see in the chief picture of the South Arch— makes it almost impossible to find a point, at sufficient distance for photographing, whence one can see clear through the bridge.   "Can't be done!" reiterated the old hermit. "Been lots of professionals here from Phœnix with their machines, and all they could get was pictures that look like caves.   You can't show through with a picture, to prove it 's a *bridge*, at all!"

But it *can* be done; and being bound to show you all that photography can possibly show of this wonder, I did it.   It cost about twenty-four solid hours of painful and perilous climbing and reconnoissance, a good deal of blood-tribute to sharp rocks and savage cactus —to whose inhospitable thorns it was necessary to cling to get footing on some of those precipices—and the camera did its work from some of the dizziest perches that tripod ever had; but here are the pictures which *do* "show through that it 's a bridge." When you look at the little far circle of light, and realize that it is two hundred feet in diameter, you will begin to feel the distance from South Arch to North Arch under that terrific rock roof.

Following up the wild bottom of the cañon from the North Arch, around gigantic boulders and under hanging cliffs, we find many other interesting things. Directly we come to "The First Tree"—one of the very largest sycamores in the United States. The cañon here is strangely picturesque. Its west wall is fifteen hundred feet high, a wilderness of splintered red granite, not perpendicular, but absolutely unscalable. The east wall is of gray limestone, perpendicular, often overhanging, but nowhere over two hundred feet high. Gowan's farm comes to the very trees that lean over its brink, and he now shows us the "lower story" of his unique homestead. Not only does his orchard stand two hundred feet in air, with room beneath for some of the largest buildings in America, but the rest of his farm is as "up-stairs," though in a different way. This fantastic east wall of the cañon is fairly honeycombed with caves, whose ghostly chambers, peopled with white visions in stone, run back unknown miles. His whole farm, his very house, is undermined by them. The old hermit has made many journeys of exploration in these caves, but has merely learned the beginning of their labyrinth. It was in one of these subterranean tours that he was lost. His torches gave out, food he had none, and for three days he faced a frightful death—their, close to his own cottage, perhaps not a hundred feet from it. From several of these caves issue fine rivulets, that coat with limestone whatever comes in their way. Some time ago Gowan's pet pig fell off the edge of the up-stairs farm, and there it lies to-day in a clear pool, pink-white as the freshest pork, but fast turning into the most durable. It is an odd fact that Pine Creek as a visible stream starts at and depends upon Gowan's farm. It is nominally Pine Creek for ten miles above, but is only a dry wash, except in time of rains; but the strong, clear stream which pours from under the South Arch of the bridge is large and permanent.

How was the bridge built? By the same peerless architect that builded the greatest wonders of the earth — the architect of the Grand Cañon and the Yellowstone, and the Yosemite — by Water. It seems probable that Gowan's little round valley was once a lake, dammed by ledges at the south end which have since disappeared. The rich alluvial soil found only here would indicate that. At all events, here was once a great round blanket of limestone, many hundred feet thick, laid down flat upon the giant lap of the granite. From unknown storage-caverns of the Mogollon watershed subterranean passages led hither, and through them flowed strong springs. In time the water — whether stored in a lake upon this limestone bench, or merely flowing over — began to burrow "short cuts" through it, as water always will in lime-rock. As the west side of the valley was lowest, there toiled the greatest throng of water-workmen. Perhaps it was a little fellow no bigger than your fist who first made passage

NATURAL BRIDGE NEAR FORT DEFIANCE, NEW MEXICO.

14

for himself through what is now the Natural Bridge. And he called his brother waters, and they crowded in after him; and each as he passed gnawed with his soft but tireless teeth at the stone, and carried his mouthful of lime-dust off down the valley, chuckling as he ran. And slowly so the tunnel grew. If men were there then, the life of generations would have seen no change; but time is the most abundant thing in creation (except for *us*); and time was there, and now the dark winding burrow of a rivulet has become one of the noblest passage-ways on earth. The hermit who owns it was born in Scotland, but has grown American in every fiber. He refuses to make a mercenary income from his wonderland. It is free for all to see—and his kindly help with it. He wants to dedicate his homestead to the government, and to have it accepted, made accessible, and cared for as a national park—as it is most worthy to be.

I often wonder if there were not great poets among the Indians of the old days. Indeed, I am sure there must have been in the race which invented the poetry of the folk-lore I have gathered among them. And when one sees amid what noblest works of Nature they lived in those days, one may well believe that bronze Homers are buried in that buried past. Science has at last learned that there can be no real study of history without consideration of physical geography as its chief factor. A race grows into character according to the country it inhabits; and the utmost savage would grow (in centuries) to be a different man when he had removed from the dull plains to the Grand Cañon, the San

Juan, Acoma, the Verde cliffs, the Tonto Basin, or any other spot where the Pueblos lived five hundred years ago. For here at the bridge they were, too. They tilled Gowan's two-story farm, and dwelt in the caves of his basement, perhaps while his ancestors were yet naked savages in old Scotia. Their rude implements and fabrics are everywhere; and among many valuable relics from that region I brought home a fetich* which is quite priceless—a symbol of the eagle holding a rattlesnake in his talons, carved from an unknown stone which baffles the file. Fancy the Pueblo boys and girls of the Dark Ages with those giant domes of the Natural Bridge for a roof to their play-ground, the Great Basin for a "swimming-hole," and miles of stalactite caves to play hide-and-seek in!

There are countless minor natural bridges in the southwest, including a very noble one in the labyrinthine cliffs of Acoma. There is a curious natural bridge near Fort Defiance, N. M. It has an arch of only about sixty feet, but is remarkable because it was carved not by water but by sand-laden winds, as are some of the most beautiful and fantastic erosions of the dry southwest.

* *Not* an idol, but the sacred symbol of some divine Power.

Thickness

THE EAGLE FETICH, ACTUAL SIZE.

SOME LEAVES FROM THE STONE AUTOGRAPH-ALBUM.

XIII.

THE STONE AUTOGRAPH-ALBUM.

AM not so sure about the present generation—
for these years on the frontier have given me
little chance to know the new boys as well as
an oldish boy would like to—but with most
young Americans of my day the autograph-
album was a cherished institution. It was a very pretty
habit, too, and a wise one, thus to press a flower from each
young friendship. Not that the autographs were always wise
—how well I remember the boys who "tried to be funny,"
and the girls who were dolefully sentimental, and the bud-
ding geniuses who tottered under thoughts palpably too
heavy for the unformed handwriting, in the thumbed red
morocco books of twenty years ago! But the older those
grimy albums grow, the more fully I feel that they were
worth while, and that it is a pity we do not keep more of
the boy "greenness" into the later years; for there are more
plants than the inanimate ones whose life is dearest and
most fragrant while they are green.

I shall never forget the supreme moments when the good
gray Longfellow and cheerful, rheumatic "Mrs. Partington"

christened my last autograph-album with their names, which were for a long time my chiefest treasures—until that dearest hero of boyhood, Captain Mayne Reid, eclipsed them all. That seems very far back; but the crowded years between, with all their adventures and dangers, have brought no keener joys. And last summer the boyish triumph came back clear and strong as ever, when I stood under one of the noblest cliffs in America and read in its vast stone pages the autographs of some of the great first heroes of the New World.

"The Stone Autograph-Album" lies in a remote and almost unknown corner of western New Mexico. It is fifty miles southwest of the Atlantic and Pacific Railroad from Grant's Station, and can be reached only by long drives through lonely but picturesque cañons and great pine forests. It is but four miles from the half-dozen Mexican houses of Las Tinajas, where the traveler can find food and shelter. The journey from the railroad is not dangerous, and need not be uncomfortable; but one should be careful to secure good horses and a guide, for the roads are not like those of the East.

Climbing and descending the long slopes of the Zuñi range, we emerge at last from the forest to a great plateau, its southeastern rim crowded with extinct volcanoes, whose somber cones explain the grim, black leagues of lava-flows that stretch everywhere. To the southwest the plateau dips into a handsome valley, guarded on the north by the wilderness of pines, and on the south by a long line of those superb mesas of many-colored sandstone which are among the characteristic beauties of the southwest. Through this valley ran an ancient and historic road—now hard to trace, for so many generations has it been abandoned—from Zuñi to the Rio Grande. Many of you have already heard something of Zuñi, that strange gray pyramid of the adobe homes of fifteen hundred Pueblo Indians. It is what is left of the famous "Seven Cities of Cibola," whose fabled gold inspired the discovery of New Mexico in 1539, and afterward the most marvelous marches of exploration ever made on this continent. Coronado, that greatest explorer, and the first Caucasian soldier who ever entered New Mexico, marched from the Gulf of California almost to where Kansas City now is, in 1540, besides making many other expeditions only less astounding. And after his day, the most of the other Spanish world-finders came first to Zuñi and thence trudged on to the Rio Grande, and to the making of a heroic history which is quite without parallel.

As we move west down the valley, the mesas grow taller and more beautiful; and presently we become aware of a noble rock which seems to be chief of all its giant brethren. Between two juniper-dotted cañons a long, wedged-shaped mesa tapers to the valley, and terminates at its edge in a magnificent cliff which bears striking resemblance to a titanic castle. Its front soars aloft in an enormous tower, and its sides are sheer walls two hundred and fifteen feet high, and thousands of feet long, with strange white battlements and wondrous shadowy bastions. Nothing without wings could mount there; but a few hundred yards south of the tower the mesa can be scaled—by a prehistoric trail of separate foot-holes worn deep in the solid rock.   At the top, we find that the wedge is hollow—a great V, in fact, for a cañon from behind splits the mesa almost to its apex.   Upon the arms of this V are the ruins of two ancient pueblos, which had been abandoned before our history began, facing each other across that fearful gulf.   These stones "cities" of the prehistoric Americans were over two hundred feet square and four or five stories tall—great terraced human beehives, with several hundred inhabitants each.

This remarkable and noble rock was known to the Spanish pioneers much more than two centuries before any of our Saxon forefathers penetrated the appalling deserts of the southwest; and even in this land full of wondrous stone monuments it was so striking that they gave it a name for its very own.   They called it *El Morro*—the Castle—and for over three hundred years it has borne that appropriate title, though the few hundred "Americans" who have seen it know it better as Inscription Rock.   It is the most precious cliff, historically, possessed by any nation on earth, and, I am ashamed to say, the most utterly uncared-for.

Lying on the ancient road from Zuñi to the river—and about thirty miles from the former—it became a most important landmark.   The necessities of the wilderness *made* it a camping-place for all who passed, since the weak spring under the shadow of that great rock was the first water in a hard day's march.   There was also plenty of wood near, and a fair shelter under the overhanging precipices. So it was that every traveler who came to the Morro in those grim centuries behind this stopped there, and that included nearly every notable figure among the first heroes who trod what is now our soil. And when they stopped, something else happened—something which occurred nowhere else in the United States, so far as we know. The sandstone of the cliff was fine and very smooth, and when the supper of jerked meat and popcorn-meal porridge had been eaten, and the mailed sentries put out to withstand the prowling Apaches, the heroes wrote their autographs upon a vast perpendicular page of stone, with their swords which had won the New World for pens!

You must not imagine that this came from the trait which gives ground for our modern rhyme about " fools' names, like their faces." These old Spaniards were as unbraggart a set of heroes as ever lived. It was not for notoriety that they wrote in that wonderful autograph-album, not in vanity, nor idly. They were piercing an unknown and frightful wilderness, in which no civilized being dwelt—a wilderness which remained until our own times the most dangerous area in America. They were few—*never* was their army over two hundred men, and sometimes it was a tenth of that—amid tens of thousands of warlike savages. The chances were a hundred to one that they would never get back to the world —even to the half-savage world of Mexico, which they had just conquered and were Christianizing. No! What they wrote was rather like leaving a headstone for unknown graves; a word to say, if any should ever follow, "Here were the men who did not come back." It was a good-by like the "Cæsar, we, who are to die, salute you."

Coronado, the first explorer, did not pass Inscription Rock, but took the southern trail from Zuñi to the wondrous cliff-city of Acoma. But among those who came after him, the road by the Morro soon became the accepted thoroughfare from Old to New Mexico; and in its mouse-colored cliffs we can read to-day many of the names that were great in the early history of America. Such queer, long names some of them are, and in such a strange, ancient hand-writing! If any boy had some of those real autographs on paper, they would be worth a small fortune; and if I were not so busy an old boy, I would trace some of them in one of my old autograph-albums, exactly as they are written in that lonely rock. But as it is, you shall have the photographic facsimiles which I made purposely for you, and do with them what you like.

On the southeast wall of the Morro are some very handsome autographs, and some very important ones. The pioneers who passed in the winter generally camped under this cliff to get the sun's warmth, while those who came in summer sought the eternal shade of the north side. All the old inscriptions are in Spanish—and many in very quaint old Spanish, of the days when spelling was a very elastic thing, and with such remarkable abbreviations as our own forefathers used as many centuries ago. All around these brave old names which are so precious to the historian—and to all who admire heroism—are Saxon names of the last few decades. Alas! some of these late-comers have been vandals, and have even erased the names of ancient heroes to make a smooth place for their "John Jones" and "George Smith." That seems to me an even more wicked and wanton thing than the chipping of historic statues for relics; and I do not, anyhow, envy the man who could write his petty name in that sacred roster.

Near the tall, lone sentinel pine which stands by the south wall of the Morro is a modest inscription of great interest and value. It is protected from the weather by a little brow of rock, and its straggling letters are legible still, though they have been there for two hundred and eighty-six years! It is the autograph of that brave soldier and wise first governor in the United States, Juan de Oñate. He was the real founder of New Mexico, since he established its government and built its first two towns. In 1598 he founded San Gabriel de los Españoles, which is the next oldest town in our country. St. Augustine, Florida, is the oldest, having been founded in 1565, also by a Spaniard. Next comes San Gabriel, and third Santa Fé, which Oñate founded in 1605. But before there was a Santa Fé, he had made a march even more wonderful than the one which brought him to New Mexico. In 1604 he trudged, at the head of thirty men, across the fearful trackless desert from San Gabriel to the Gulf of California, and back again! And on the return from that marvelous "journey to discover the South Sea" (the Pacific) he camped at the Morro and wrote in its eternal

15

page. Here it is, just as he wrote it two years before our Saxon forefathers had built a hut in America, even on the sea-coast—while he was fifteen hundred miles from the ocean. The inscriptions are nearly all of such antique lettering, and so full of abbreviations, that I shall give you the Spanish

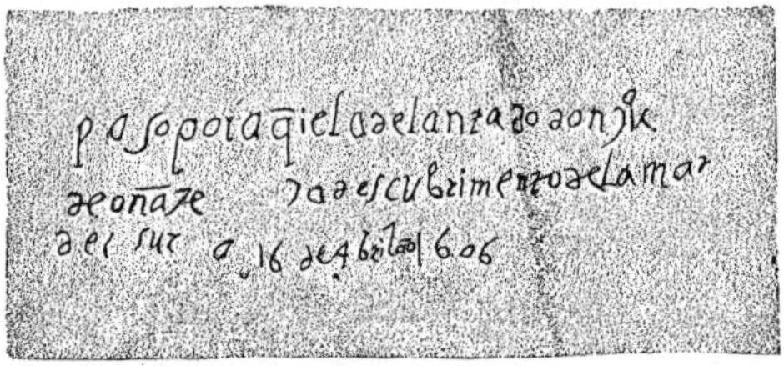

FIG. I.   JUAN DE OÑATE.

text in type with an interlined translation, so that you may pick out the queerly written words and get an idea of sixteenth and seventeenth century "short-hand." Oñate's legend reads:

" *Pasó por aqui el adelantado* * *don Jua de Oñate al descubri-*
      Passed by here the   officer   Don Juan de Oñate to the discov-
mento de la mar del sur á 16 de Abril āo. 1605."
      ery   of the sea of the South on the 16th of April, year 1605.

This is the oldest identified autograph on the Rock except one, which is not absolutely certain—that of Pedro Romero; his date reads apparently 17580. Either some one has foolishly added the nought—which is very improbable—or the 1 is simply an *i*, and the supposed 7 an old-fashioned 1.

---

* We have no exact word for *adelantado*. He was the officer in command of a new country.

This is very likely. "And" — *y* or *i*, in Spanish — was often written before the year; and the chances are that this inscription means "Pedro Romero and 1580." In that case, Romero was one of the eight companions with whom Francisco Sanchez Chamuscado made his very remarkable march of exploration in that year.

Just below Oñate's autograph is one which some careless explorers have made eighty years earlier than his. The second figure in the date *does* look like a 5; but no white man had ever seen any part of New Mexico in 1526; and the figure is really an old-style 7. The autograph is that of Basconzelos, and reads:

" Por aqui pazó el Alferes D^n Joseph de Payba Basconzelos el
By here passed the Ensign Don Joseph de Payba Basconzelos, the
año que trujo el Cavildo del Reyno á su costa á 18 de Febo de
year that he brought the town-council of the kingdom (N. M.) at his own expense
1726 anos."
on the 18th of Feb., of 1726 years (the year 1726).

Not far away is the pretty autograph of Diego de Vargas — that dashing but generous general who reconquered New Mexico after the fearful Pueblo Indian rebellion of 1680. In that rebellion twenty-one gentle missionaries and four hundred other Spaniards were massacred by the Indians in one day, and the survivors were driven back into Old Mexico. This inscription was written when Vargas made his first dash back into New Mexico — a prelude to the years of terrific fighting of the Reconquest. He wrote:

" Aqui estaba el Genl. Dn. Do. de Vargas, quien conquistó á
Here was the General Don Diego de Vargas, who conquered for

nuestra Santa Fé y á la Real Corona todo el Nuevo Mexico á su
our Holy Faith and for the Royal Crown (of Spain) all the New Mexico, at his
costa, año de 1692."
own expense (in the) year of 1692.

A little north of Vargas's valuable inscription is that (figure 2) of the expedition sent by Governor Francisco Martinez de Baeza to arrange the troubles in Zuñi, on the urgent request of the chief missionary Fray Cristobal de Quirós. It reads:

" *Pasamos por aqui el sargento mayor, y el capitan Jua. de*
We pass by here, the lieutenant-colonel, and the Captain Juan de
Arechuleta, y el aiudante Diego Martin Barba, y el Alferes
Arechuleta, and the lieutenant Diego Martin Barba, and the Ensign
Agostyn de Ynojos, año de 1636."
Augustin de Ynojos, in the year of 1636.

Below this are some ancient Indian pictographs. The *sargento mayor* (literally "chief sergeant") who is not named

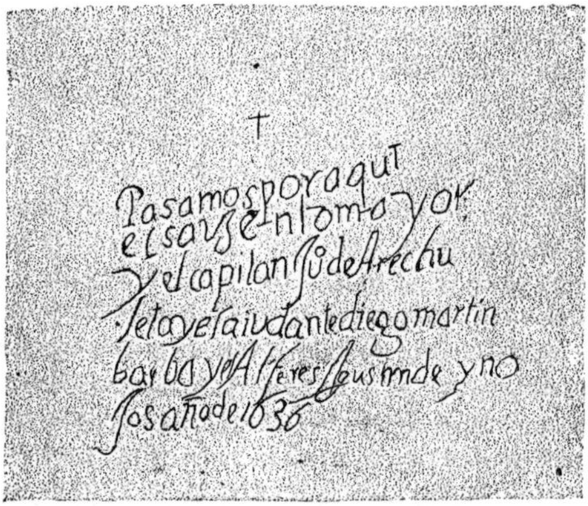

FIG. 2.　DIEGO MARTIN BARBA AND ALFERES AGOSTYN.

was probably brave Francisco Gomez. The inscription is in the handwriting of Diego Martin Barba, who was the official secretary of Governor Baeza. In a little cavity near by is the inscription of "Juan Garsya, 1636." He was a member of the same expedition. The handsome autograph of Ynojos appears in several places on the rock.

Two quaint lines, in tiny but well-preserved letters, recall a pathetic story. It is that of a poor common soldier, who did not write his year. But history supplies that.

"*Soy de mano de Felipe de Arellano á 16 de Setiembre,*
I am from the hand of Felipe de Arellano, on the 16th of September,
soldado."
soldier.

He was one of the Spanish "garrison" of *three men* left to guard far-off Zuñi, and slain by the Indians in the year 1700. Not far away is the autograph of the leader of the "force" of six men who went in 1701 from Santa Fé to Zuñi (itself a desert march of three hundred miles) to avenge that massacre, the Captain Juan de Urribarri. He left merely his name.

An autograph nearly obliterated is that of which we can still read only:

"*Pasó por aqui Fran⁰. de An . . . Alma . . .*"

This was Francisco de Anaia Almazan, a minor but heroic officer who served successively under Governor Otermin, the great soldier Cruzate, and the Reconqueror Vargas, and was in nearly every action of the long, red years of the Pueblo Rebellion. At the time of the great massacre in 1680, he was in the pueblo of Santa Clara. His three companions were

butchered by the savages, and Almazan escaped alone by
swimming the Rio Grande. He probably wrote in the album
of the Morro in 1692, at the same time with De Vargas. Another autograph of a member of the same expedition is that
of Diego Lucero de Godoy (figure 3). He was then a *sargento mayor*, a very good and brave officer, who was with
Governor Otermin in the bloody siege of Santa Fé by the
Indians, and in that dire retreat when the bleeding Spaniards
hewed their way through the swarming beleaguers and fought

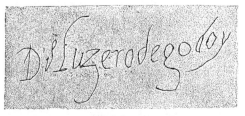

FIG. 3.   DIEGO LUCERO DE GODOY.

a passage to El Paso. He was also in nearly every battle of
the Reconquest. Salvador Holguin, whose autograph is also
on the rock, was another of Vargas's soldiers. Of about the
same time were several Naranjos, of whom Joseph was the
first *alcalde mayor* (about equivalent to district judge) of
Zuñi after the Reconquest. Of a much earlier date was the
unknown soldier "Juan Gonzales, 1629" (figure 4). A subsequent Gonzales passed and wrote here seventy-one years later,
in a very peculiar "fist":

> "*Pasé por aquy el año 1700 yo, Ph. Gonzales.*"
> I passed by here (in) the year 1700, I, Felipe Gonzales.

FIG. 4.   JUAN GONZALES.

A *firma* as peculiar as that of our own famous "puzzler,"
General Spinner, is appended to the entry (figure 5):

" *A 5 del mes de Junyo deste año de 1709 pasó por aquy para*
On the 5th of the month of June of this year of 1709 passed by here, bound

Zuñi Ramon Paez Jurt'do."
for Zuñi, Ramon Paez Hurtado.

FIG. 5.   RAMON PAEZ HURTADO.

Another Hurtado wrote on the other wall, in queer little square characters (figure 6) :

"*El dia 14 de Julio de 1736 pasó por aqui el Gen¹ Juan Paez*
(On) the day 14th of July of 1736 passed by here the General Juan Paez
Hurtado, Visitador — y en su compañia el cabo Joseph Truxillo."
Hurtado, Official Inspector, and in his company the corporal Joseph Truxillo.

This one was a son of the *great* General Hurtado — the bosom friend of Vargas, repeatedly lieutenant-governor of the territory, and in 1704 acting governor. He was afterward greatly persecuted by Governors Cubero and Martinez. The son also was a general, but not so prominent as his father.

FIG. 6.　JUAN PAEZ HURTADO.

On the north side of the Morro are the longest and most elaborate inscriptions, the rock being there more favorable. The earliest of them are the two long legends of the then governor of New Mexico, Don Francisco Manuel de Silva Nieto. They were not written by him, but by some admiring officer in his little force. A part has been effaced by the modern vandal, but enough remains to mark that very notable journey. The first says (figure 7) :

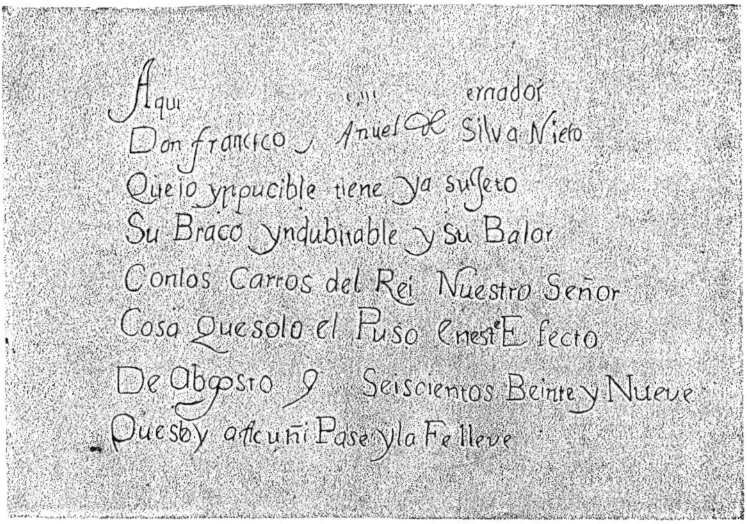

FIG. 7. DON FRANCISCO MANUEL DE SILVA NIETO.

"*Aqui* . . . [*pasó el Gober*] *nador Don Francico Manuel de*
  Here   passed the Governor Don Francisco Manuel de
Silva Nieto que lo ynpucible tiene ya sujeto su Braco yndubitable
Silva Nieto that the impossible has already (been) effected (by) his arm indom-
y su Balor, con los Carros del Rei Nuestro Señor; cosa que solo
itable and his valor, with the wagons of the King Our Master; a thing which
el Puso en este Efecto, de Abgosto 9,   Seiscientos   Beinte   y
only he put in this shape on August 9, (one thousand) six hundred, twenty and
Neuve, que . . . á Cuñi Pasé y la Fé llevé."
nine, that   to Zuñi I passed and the Faith carried.

What is meant by Governor Nieto's "carrying the faith"
(that is, Christianity) is that on this expedition he took along
the heroic priests who established the mission of Zuñi, and
who labored alone amid that savage flock.

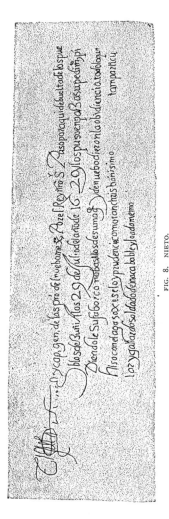

FIG. 8. NIETO.

Nieto's other inscription (figure 8), written on another journey, is in a more characteristic handwriting. It says:

"*El Illustrisimo Señor y*
The most Illustrious Sir and
Cap. gen. de las pros. del
Captain-General of the provinces of
nuebo Mexco. Por el Rey nro.
the New Mexico for the King Our Mas-
Sr. Pasó por aqui de buelta de
ter, passed by here on the return from
los pueblos de Zuñi á los 29 de
the villages of Zuñi on the 29th of
Julio del año de 1629; y los
July of the year of 1629 and them (the
puso en paz á su pendimto.,
Indians) ne put in peace at their
pidiendole su fabor como ba-
request, (they) asking his favor as
sallos de su mag^d. *Y de nuebo*
vassals of His Majesty. And anew
dieron la obediencia; todo lo
they gave obedience; all of which
que hiso con el agasaxe, selo, y
he did with persuasiveness, zeal and
prudencia, como tan christian-
prudence, like such a most Chris-
isimo . . . tam particular y
tian,   such a careful and
gallardo soldado de inacabable
gallant   soldier   of   tireless
y . . . memoria . . ."
and   memory . . ."

Another long inscription, not so handsomely written but very characteristic, is that of Governor Martinez, near by:

"*Año de 1716 á los 26 de Agosto paso por aqui Don Feliz*
(In the) year of 1716 on the 26th of August, passed by here Don Feliz
Martinez, Govern^r. y Cap^n. Genl. de este Reyno, á la reduczion
Martinez, Governor and Captain-General of this Kingdom, to the reduction
y conq^{ta}. de Moqui; y en su compañia el Rdo. P. F. Antonio
and conquest of Moqui; and in his company the Reverend Father Fray Antonio
Camargo, Custodio y Juez Eclesiastico."
Camargo, Custodian and Judge-Ecclesiastic.

This was an expedition to reclaim to Christianity the lofty cliff-built pueblos of Moqui, which had slain their missionaries; but it signally failed, and Martinez was recalled in disgrace from his governorship. He and Pedro Rodriguez Cubero were the worst governors New Mexico ever had after 1680, and no one was sorry for him. The *Custodio* was the local head of the Church in New Mexico. A curious flourish at the end of his autograph is the *rubrica* much affected by writers of the past centuries. There are many characteristic *rubricas* among the names on the Morro.

The first visit of a bishop to the southwest is recorded in a very clear inscription, which runs:

"*Dia 28 de Sept. de 1737 años llegó aqui el Illmo.*
(On the) day 28th of September of 1737 years, reached here the most illus-
Sr. Dr. Dn. Mrn. De Elizaecochea, Obpo. de Durango, y el
trious Sir Doctor Don Martin de Elizaecochea, Bishop of Durango, and (on) the
dia 29 pasó á Zuñi."
day 29th went on to Zuñi.

New Mexico belonged to the bishopric of Durango (Mexico) until 1852. A companion autograph is that of the "Bachiller" (Bachelor of Arts) Don Ygnacio de Arrasain. He was with the bishop on this journey—an arduous and dangerous journey, even a century later than 1737.

One of the most puzzling inscriptions in this precious autograph album, and a very important one, is that of the soldier Lujan (figure 9). It is almost in hieroglyphics, and was never deciphered until I put it into the hands of a great

FIG. 9.   LUJAN.

student of ancient writings—though after he solved the riddle it is clear enough to any one who knows Spanish. Its violent abbreviations, the curious capitals with the small final letters piled "overhead," and its reference to a matter of history of which few Americans ever heard, combined to keep it long a mystery. Reduced to long-hand Spanish, it reads:

" *Se pasaron á 23 de Marzo de 1632 años á la benganza de*
They passed on the 23d of March of 1632 years to the avenging of the
Muerte del Padre Letrado.   *Lujan.*"
death of the Father Letrado.

What a romance and what a tragedy are hidden in those two lines! Father Francisco Letrado was the first permanent missionary to the strange pyramid-pueblo of Zuñi. He came to New Mexico about 1628, and was first a missionary to the Jumanos—the tattooed savages who lived in the edge of the great plains, east of the Rio Grande. In 1629, you will remember, the mission of Zuñi was founded, and he was sent to that lone, far parish and to his death. He labored earnestly with his savage flock, but not for long. In February, 1630, they mercilessly slew him. Francisco de la Mora Ceballos was then Governor of New Mexico, and he sent this expedition "to avenge Father Letrado's death," under the lead of the *maestro de campo* (Colonel) Tomas de Albizu. Albizu performed his mission successfully and without bloodshed. The Zuñis had retreated to the top of their thousand-foot cliff, the To-yo-ál-la-na, but were induced to return peaceably to their pueblos. Lujan was a soldier of the expedition.

There are a great many other old Spanish autographs on the sheer walls of the Morro; but these are the principal ones so far deciphered. Of the American names only two or three are of any note at all. The earliest date from 1849, and are those of Lieutenant Simpson and his scientific companion Kern—doubtless the first of us to visit the spot. All the other Saxon names are very recent and very unimportant.

I am sure that if any of my readers had any one of those old autographs in his album, he would guard it jealously; and it is a shame that we are neglecting that noble stone

16

book of the Morro. A few more years and a few more vandals, and nothing will be left of what now makes the rock
so precious. The government should protect it, as it would
be protected in any other civilized land; and when some of
you get into Congress, I hope you will look to this and other
such duties. Otherwise the next generation will awake only
to find that it has lost a unique and priceless treasure.

XIV.

F a line were drawn from Lake Manitoba to the Gulf of Mexico at Galveston, approximately halving the United States, and we could get these two halves on a small enough scale to compare them side by side, we should find that Nature herself had already made as striking a division. We should find such a difference between them as we now scarcely realize. Broadly speaking, we should discover the eastern half to be low, rather flat, wooded and wet; the western half many times as high above sea-level, extremely mountainous, generally bare, and phenomenally dry. Its landscapes are more brown than green, its ranges barren and far more bristling than those of the east; and its plains vast bleak uplands. Its very air is as different from that of the eastern half as white is different from gray. It is many times lighter and many times clearer, and incomparably drier. It is a sort of wizard air, which plays all sorts of good-natured tricks upon the stranger. Delicious to breathe, a real tonic to the lungs, a stimulant to the skin, it seems to delight in fooling the eyes. Through its magic clearness one sees three times as far as in the heavier atmosphere of the east, and the stranger's estimates of distance have all to be made over. It is no uncommon thing for the traveler to deem an object but five miles off when it is really twenty miles or even more. And a still more startling trick of this strange atmosphere is that it very frequently makes one see things which do not exist at all! It is a curious paradox that this atmospheric freak, of which you know as the mirage, is confined to dry countries—deserts, in fact—and that the illusion it most commonly presents is water! Towns and mountains and animals are sometimes pictured, but oftenest it is a counterfeit of water that is shown the weary traveler in a land where there is no water, and where water means life.

The very landscape under this wonderful air has an appearance to be found nowhere else. Its barrenness seems enchanted; and there is an unearthly look about it all. Watercourses are extremely rare — in a quarter of a continent there are only three good-sized rivers, and it is in places hundreds of miles between brooks. In a word, the country seems to have been burnt out—it reminds one of a gigantic cinder.

It is true that there are in this area a great many rivers of a sort not to be found in the East—and such strange rivers! They are black as coal, and full of strange, savage waves, and curious curling eddies, and enormous bubbles. The springs from which they started ran dry centuries ago; a mouth not one of them ever had; and yet their black flood has not been soaked up by the thirsty sands. There lies the broad, wild current, sometimes thirty feet higher than its banks, yet not overflowing them; a current across which men walk without danger of sinking, but not without danger of another sort; a current in which not fishes but wild beasts live—often even one river on top of another!

You will wonder what sort of rivers these can be. They are characteristic of the West—there are none of them in the East; but in an area larger than that which holds three-fourths of the population of the United States they are a part of the country. They line hundreds of valleys. If the rest of the landscape suggests fire, they suggest it ten times more. And rightly enough, for they have seen fire—nay, they have *been* fire. They are burnt rivers, that ran as fire and remain as stone.

By this time you will have guessed what I mean—that these rivers of stone are neither more nor less than lava-flows. They are stranger than that African river of ink (made by the combination of chemicals soaked from the soil), and incomparably more important, for they have to do with causes which much more nearly affect mankind. The great difference between the East and West is that the latter is a volcanic country, while the former is not; and nearly all the striking dissimilarities of air, climate, landscape, and even customs of the people, arise from this fact. The West has been heaved up by the fires within, and burned out and parched dry—so dry that even the sky feels it. The rainfall is far less than in the East; and to make their crops grow the western farmers have to flood their fields several times in a season from some stream or reservoir.

As we go south this volcanic condition becomes more and more predominant. The vast southwest is a strongly volcanic country, and covered with embers of its old fires. There are no active volcanoes in the United States, but in the southwest there are thousands of extinct ones, each with its one to a dozen black rivers of stone. These volcanoes are not large peaks like the giants of Central and South America; most of them are small cones rising but little above the surrounding plains, some not more than fifty feet. Yet so elevated is the whole country there that the top of such a cone is frequently much higher above the sea-level than the summit of Mount Washington.

Of the many volcanic regions I have explored, one of the most interesting is in the Zuñi Mountains of western New Mexico, and along their slopes. All through the range—whose tops are over eight thousand feet in altitude—are scattered scores of extinct volcanoes; and their lava-flows have overrun many thousands of square miles. The range is covered with a magnificent pine forest—a rare enough thing in the southwest—partly growing upon ancient flows, and cut in all directions by later ones. The soil everywhere is sown with jagged fragments of lava, which makes travel irksome; and in the picturesque Zuñi cañon which traverses the range is a singular sight—where the lava, too impatient to await outlet by a crater, boiled out in great waves from under the bottom of the cañon's walls, which are sandstone precipices hundreds of feet high.

The largest crater in this range is about two miles south

of the lonely little ranch-house at Agua Fria. It is a great, reddish-brown, truncated cone, rising about five hundred feet above the plateau, and from three sides looks very regular and round. Around it are the tall pines, and a few have even straggled up its sides, as if to see what it all means. But they have found it hard climbing, and cling upon its precipitous flanks as if disheartened and out of breath. Nor can one blame them. To the top of that crater is one of the very hardest climbs I know—the ascent of Pike's Peak did not tire me nearly so much. The whole cone is covered several feet deep with coarse, sharp volcanic ashes, or rather cinders—for each fragment is as large as the tip of one's finger. The slope is of extreme steepness, and this loose covering of scoriæ makes ascent almost hopeless. The climber sinks calf-deep at every step; and, worse still, at every step sets the whole face of the slope, for a rod around, to sliding down-hill. No one can go straight up that arduous pitch; one has to climb sidewise and in zigzags, and with frequent pauses for breath; and it is a decided relief, mental as well as physical, when one stands at last upon the rim of that giant bowl.

A strange, wild sight it is when we gain the edge of the crater. A fairly terrific abyss yawns beneath us; an abyss of dizzy depth and savage grandeur. Its bottom is far lower than the level of the country around the outside of the cone —from that rim to the bottom of the crater must be eight hundred feet. In shape the interior is less like a great bowl than a great funnel. The rim is very narrow—in many

places not more than six feet across—and terribly rough.
The rock is cooked to an absolute cinder, and is more
jagged than anything familiar to the East.   Imagine a million tons of rock exactly like one great "clinker" from a
furnace, and you get some idea of it.   Tall, weird cliffs of the
same roasted rock surround the crater a few hundred feet
below the rim; and below these again is the long, swift slope
of scoriæ to the V-shaped bottom.   Under the eastern cliff
is a strange, misplaced little grove of cotton-woods, which
seem ill enough at ease in that gruesome spot—their roots
clutching amid the ashy rocks, their tops hundreds of feet
below the rim.   Here and there in the cliffs are wild, dark-
mouthed caves; and from these long, curious lines lead
across the slope of cinders.   They look like tracks across a
sand-bank—and tracks they are, though one would never
look for footprints in such a forbidding chasm.   But, oddly
enough, this dead crater is the chosen retreat of more than
one form of life.   There are no other cotton-woods in a great
many miles except those I have mentioned—outside the
crater it is too cold for this shivering tree.   And this same
grim shelter has been chosen by one of the least delicate of
animals—for those tracks are bear-tracks.   Several of these
big brutes live in the caves of the crater and of the lava-flows
outside.   The Agua Fria region is a great place for bear;
and at certain times of the year they are an enormous nui-
sance to the people at the rancho, actually tearing down
quarters of beef hung against the house, and very nearly
tearing down the house with the meat.   Several have been

killed right at the house. A few days before my last visit to
the crater one of the cowboys, a powerful young Ute Indian,
was herding the horses near the foot of the cone, when he saw
a huge black bear scrambling up the acclivity. A good shot
at nearly five hundred yards brought Bruin rolling to the
foot of the cone, quite dead. His skin was an imposing sight
when tacked upon the outside of the log-house to dry, for it
reached from the ridge-pole to the ground, and then had several inches to spare. Besides the bears, the coyotes, wild-cats,
and mountain-lions which infest that region, all make their
homes in the caves of the *mal pais* or "bad lands," the general name in New Mexico for lava and other volcanic areas.
It is noticeable that only such animals as these and the dog
—some creature with cushioned feet—can live or travel in
the *mal pais*. Anything with hoofs, like the deer or antelope
which abound there, or the cattle and sheep which also range
those mountains, cannot long tread those savage-edged rocks.

The funnel of the crater is not perfect. On the south side
the huge bowl has lost part of its rim. The crater is about
seven hundred yards across the top, and nearly three hundred yards deep; and you may imagine that it was a rather
warm and weird time when this great caldron was full to
the brim with *boiling rock*. A terrific potful it must have
been, and doubly fearful when that stupendous weight burst
out the side of the pot and poured and roared down the valley a flood of fire. Think of a lake of lava so heavy that it
simply tore out a mountain-side eight hundred feet high and
five hundred feet thick at the bottom! The break in the

crater is in the shape of a huge irregular V, nearly a thousand feet across the top, and over five hundred from top to
bottom; and all that great slice of solid rock, weighing mill-
ions of tons (for it takes only a cubic yard to weigh a ton),
was knocked out as unceremoniously as though a giant had
cleft it out with an ax.

That is the sort of spring in which the rivers of stone had
their source; and this particular crater fed many enormous
streams. Of course it is many centuries since this grim
spring ran dry; but we can judge very well how it acted when
it sent out its strange hot floods. First, above the soughing
of the pines rose deep, pent-up rumblings, and the solid earth
rocked and shivered. Then there was a great explosion just
where that still brown cone stands to-day, and this great wart
was heaved up from the level plateau, and a vast cloud of
steam and ashes sprung far into the sky. Then the molten
flood of rock rose in the great bowl, and brimmed it, and ran
over in places, and boiled and seethed. And suddenly, with
a report louder than a hundred cannon, the wall of the crater
broke, and that resistless deluge of fire rolled like an avalanche down the valley, plowing a channel fifty feet deep in
the bed-rock at its outlet, mowing down giant pines as if
they had been straws, sweeping along enormous boulders like
driftwood, and spreading death and eternal desolation for
leagues around. A flood of any sort is a fearful thing. I
have seen a wall of water ninety feet high sweep down a narrow pass, at the bursting of a great reservoir at Worcester,
Mass. It cut off oak-trees two feet in diameter and left

of them only square, splintered stumps. A five-story brick
building stood in the way, and quicker than you could snap
a finger it was not. Iron pipes that weighed a thousand
pounds *floated* on that mad flood for a moment! And what
must it be when the breaking dam lets out an avalanche of
molten rock in a wave five hundred feet high!

That first outrush must have been a sublime thing. But
even more than water, a lava stream begins to lose force as
it gets away from its head. It is so much thicker than water
at the start, and with every mile it grows thicker still. Soon
it runs very much like cold molasses; a sluggish, black, un-
natural sort of stream, with its middle higher than its sides
and the sides higher than the banks. The process of cooling
begins very quickly and goes on rapidly. The "river" runs
more and more slowly; and along its upper course (if the
eruption has ceased) a shell will begin to form within a fort-
night. So here is the strange phenomenon of a river running
inside a stone conduit of its own making. The shell becomes
hard enough, long before it is cool enough, to walk upon;
and within, the fiery flood still pours along. A great deal of
gas and steam is imprisoned in the molten flow. Sometimes
it only makes huge bubbles, which remain frozen in the eternal stone. I have found these bubbles ten feet in diameter
— curious arched caves, in which a whole party might camp.
But if the volume of gas be too great, terrific explosions occur; and in places the top of the flow for a hundred acres is
rent into a million fragments, so sharp-pointed that no creature can cross them.

The chief river of stone from this crater is about fifty-seven miles long, and its black, unmoving flood covers some four hundred square miles. It runs south for a few miles from the crater, then makes a great bend to the east, and, passing the beautiful *rincon** of Cebollita, runs to the northeast nutil it unites with a smaller flow in the valley of the San José. In places it is a dozen miles wide, and in some narrow passes not more than a mile. At the bend the hot, sluggish current actually ran a couple of miles up-hill, in its reluctance to turn a corner.

Not far from this elbow in the stone river is a very interesting spot. The Pueblo Indians have dwelt for unknown ages in that part of New Mexico; and on a fine rock bluff at Cebollita is one of the handsomest of their prehistoric ruins —a large stone pueblo surrounded by a noble stone wall. This fortified town was already deserted and forgotten when Coronado came in 1540. The Quéres Pueblos have still a legend of the *Año de la Lumbre*, or "Year of Fire." They say their forefathers dwelt in these valleys when the lava floods came and made it so hot that all had to move away; and there is a dumb but eternal witness to the truth of their story. A few miles from Cebollita were some of their small, separate farm-houses in the pretty valley, and through one of these a current of the stone river ran. There stands to this day that ancient house, long roofless but with strong walls still; and through a gap in them and over the floor lies the frozen black tide.

There are two islands in this peculiar river, and as peculiar

* Corner.

as itself. Instead of rising above the flood they are below it
—lonely parks with grass and stately pines, walled with the
black lava which stands twenty feet above their level. The
largest of these parks contains about twenty thousand acres.
There is a narrow trail into it, and it is used as a pasture for
the horses of the ninety-seven-thousand-acre A. L. C. ranch.
There are only two trails by which this lava-flow can be
crossed by men or horses. Everywhere else it is as much as
one's life is worth to attempt a passage. No one inexperi-
enced can conceive of the cruel roughness of these flows. The
strongest shoes are absolutely cut to pieces in a short walk;
and then woe to the walker if he have not arrived at more
merciful ground. Several years ago a band of horse-thieves,
led by a desperado known as Charlie Ross, were fleeing from
Gallup with several stolen animals. The officers were close at
their heels, and to be overtaken meant a swift bullet or a
long rope. The "rustlers" missed the trail, but tried to cross
a narrow part of the flow. It was a cruel and indescribable
passage. They got across and escaped—for the pursuers
were not so foolhardy as to enter the lava—but on foot.
Their horses, including a four-hundred-dollar thoroughbred,
were no longer able to stand. The desperate riders had
spurred them over that cruel surface until their hoofs were
absolutely *gone*, and the poor brutes had no feet at all! The
robbers themselves came out barefoot, and the rocks were
marked with their blood. I am glad to remember that the
pursuers soon got around the *mal pais*, and put the horses
out of their misery.

17

This flow runs for several miles beside the track of the Atlantic and Pacific Railway, just west of McCarty, and comes to an abrupt end in a pretty little meadow there. The small bluish San José creek rises in a cold spring which pours forth from a cave in the lava, very much like the beautiful spring at Agua Fria. The creek evidently belonged in the valley before the lava came, and despite that fearful invasion of fire it still holds its own. For miles it runs through the great black river of stone, now in winding channels, and again heard but unseen in long caves under the lava. There are also in this part of the flow a dozen or more nearly circular basins, some filled with water from the brook, and a favorite breeding-place for wild ducks. It is a very unsatisfactory place to hunt, however, for your duck is very liable to fall into one of the deep, narrow cracks in the lava, where he is lost forever.

The wildest and most interesting part of this stone river is up near its head. Everywhere it keeps its old waves and its very eddies, frozen into enduring rock; everywhere it has its upheavals and its dangerous fissures. But near the crater its surface is inconceivably wild and broken. It seems to have gouged out a tremendous channel for itself in its first mad rush. For a mile the flow is a succession of " slumps." The solid rock beneath seems to have dropped out of sight, and when the fiery river cooled it dropped too, but only in places. I suppose that really the molten lava all ran out from that part of the conduit, and that finally the shell broke down in spots. But what a conduit it must have been!

For areas of five acres of this hardest rock, twenty feet thick, have simply dropped down and lie at the bottom of a savage well seventy-five feet deep! There are a dozen or more of these wild "sink-holes," varying from half an acre in area to more than ten times as much; and they are the most forbidding, desolate, chaotic wrecks imaginable. Most of them are inaccessible, for their rock walls are sheer; but I have clambered down into some of them, and in every one which could be entered have found the dens of bears and other wild beasts. They are safe enough there from molestation even by the ubiquitous cowboy, who has to ride everywhere else in search of stray cattle.

In one of these sinks I made a curious discovery in the fall of 1891. Perpetual snow is supposed not to exist in the southwest. We have several peaks over twelve thousand feet high, but that is not a sufficient altitude for eternal snow in this arid climate. The spring sun makes short work of the drifts, even at the greatest elevations. But here I found perpetual snow at an altitude of eight thousand feet, in the strangest refrigerator nature ever built.

It was in the largest of these sinks near the Agua Fria crater — a gruesome pit into which I descended with some misgivings, in quest of bear, and in company with the Ute cowboy. After exploring the various caves in vain, finding plenty of traces of bear but no bear, we went clambering over the chaos of lava blocks to a great, dark cavity at the head of the sink. Here the broken conduit showed plainly. It is a huge tunnel, with an arch of nearly fifty feet, and running

back under the lava no one knows how far. In the mouth
of the tunnel, fully one hundred feet below the surface of the
flow, is a clear, cold pool of water, walled behind by a bank
of snow twenty feet in visible thickness. It is flat as a floor
on top, and sheer as a wall in front, and runs back nearly a
hundred feet. The successive deposits are clearly marked. In
the severe winter of those mountains a great deal of snow
drifts into the tunnel. In summer this settles and hardens,
and volcanic ashes blow in and form a thin layer upon it.
The sun never enters beyond a point about ten feet back of a
perpendicular from the top of the cliff, and as the cliff forms
a sort of bay, this mass of snow is touched by the sun in a
semicircle, and melts so that its face is in the shape of a crescent. This perpendicular wall of snow twenty feet high is
very pretty, for, with its bluish strata interlined with the yellow horizontal bands of dust, it looks for all the world like a
huge section of Mexican onyx. It is settled and solidified
until it is half ice; but the hottest summer makes no further impression upon it. A strange place for eternal snow,
truly; a novel idea in ice-houses—this refrigerator in what
was once the hottest place in the world! The contrast is
noticeable enough, even now. In summer the sun beats
down into the pit with great fury, and the black rocks ab-
sorb its heat until a hand can hardly be laid upon them.
But the instant one steps into the shade of the great arch
there is a tremendous change in temperature. From being
nearly broiled one passes in two steps to a chill which cannot long be borne. Up under the gloomy rock arch twitter-

ing swallows have their nests, and all the hot day they skim about in the mouth of the tunnel, now in sun and now in shade.

Such volcanic ice-houses are sometimes useful, too. The city of Catania in Sicily is supplied with ice from a somewhat similar cavern in one of the lava-flows of Ætna. But I do not know how the ice-cave of the Zuñi Mountains can ever be made available, unless, indeed, the resident bears and wild-cats should take a notion to drag in a calf or deer and keep it in this unique cold-storage warehouse against a possible famine.

Not only are there these stone rivers in so many of the valleys, but thousands of the great sandstone mesas (table-lands) of New Mexico and Arizona are capped with flat lava-flows from ten to fifty feet thick. In some places there are solitary buttes, one or two hundred feet high, standing alone in a plain. Their tops are solid lava, but there is not another sign of a flow for miles around. Those flows were extremely ancient, and erosion has cut down all the rest of the lava-covered upland and carried it away in sand, leaving only this one strange "island" in token of what once was. Very frequently, too, in such a mesa the underlying sandstone is so much softer that it has been worn away first, and the harder cap of lava projects everywhere like a great, rough cornice.

XV

THE NAVAJO BLANKET.

NE of the striking curiosities of one of our Strange Corners is the Navajo blanket. There is no other blanket like it. It is remarkable that half-naked savages in a remote wilderness which is almost a desert, unwashed nomads who never live in a house, weave a handsomer, more durable, and more valuable blanket than is turned out by the costly and intricate looms of Europe and America; but it is true. The covers which shelter us nights are very poor affairs, artistically and commercially, compared to those superb fabrics woven by Navajo women in the rudest caricature of a loom. Blanket-weaving is the one domestic industry of this great tribe of twenty thousand souls, whose temporary brush shelters dot the northwestern mountains of New Mexico and the eastern ranges of Arizona; but they do it well. The work of the men is stock-raising — they have a million and a half of sheep, a hundred thousand cattle, and several hundred thousand beautiful ponies — and they also plant a very little corn. The women have no housework to do, because they have no houses — a very different social condition from that of their neighbors, the cleanly, industrious, farm-tending, home-loving Pueblos. They make hardly any pottery, buying what they need from the expert Pueblos, in exchange for their own matchless blankets, which the Pueblos no longer weave.

The Navajo country is a very lonely and not altogether safe one, for these Indians are jealous of intruders; but it is full of interest, and there is much to be seen in safe proximity to the railroad—particularly near Manuelito, the last station in New Mexico.

It fairly takes one's breath away to ride up one of these barren mesas, among the twisted piñons, and find a ragged Indian woman squatted before a loom made of three sticks, a rope, and a stone, weaving a blanket of great beauty in design and color, and with the durability of iron. But that is what one may see a thousand times in this strange territory by taking the necessary trouble, though it is a sight that few white people do see. The Navajo is a seeker of seclusion, and instinctively pitches his camp in an out-of-the-way location. You may pass within fifty yards of his *hogan* and never suspect the proximity of human life, unless your attention is called by one of his wolfish dogs, which are very fond of strangers—and strangers *raw*. If you can induce the dog to save you for supper, and will follow his snarling retreat, this is what you may see:

Under the shelter of a juniper, a semicircular wind-break built breast-high of brush, and about fifteen feet from point to point; a tiny heap of smoldering coals; a few greasy sheep-skins and blankets lying against the brush; perhaps

the jerked meat of a sheep hanging to a branch, and near it
pendent a few silver ornaments; a bottle-necked basket,
pitched without and full of cold water; an old Spencer
carbine or a Winchester leaning against the "wall"; a few
bare-legged youngsters of immeasurable mirth, but diffident
toward strangers; mayhap the lord of the castle and a male
companion or two playing *cunquian* with solemn faces and
Mexican cards; the dogs, the lariated ponies—*and* the lady
of the house at her remarkable loom.

For simplicity of design, the Navajo "loom"—if it can be
dignified by such a title—is unique.   Occasionally the frame
is made by setting two posts firmly in the ground about six
feet apart, and lashing cross-pieces at top and bottom.   So
complicated an affair as this, however, is not usual.   Ordi-
narily a straight pole is lashed between two trees, at a height
of five or six feet from the ground.   A strong rawhide rope,
wound loosely round and round this, serves to suspend the
"supplementary yarn-beam," a straight bar of wood five or
six feet long.   To this in turn is attached a smaller bar,
around which the upper ends of the stout strings which con-
stitute the warp are tied.   The lower ends of these strings
are tied to a similar bar, which is anchored by stones at a
distance of about two inches from the ground, thus keeping
the string taut.   And there is your loom.

On the ground a foot away squats the weaver, bare-shinned
and bare-armed, with her legs crossed tailor fashion.   The
warp hangs vertically before her, and she never rises while
weaving.   A stick holds the alternate cords of the warp

apart in opposite directions, and thus enables her to run the successive threads of the woof across without difficulty. As soon as a thread has been thus loosely introduced to its proper position, she proceeds to ram it down with the tightness of the charge in a Fourth-of-July cannon by means of a long, thin, hard-wood "batten-stick," frequently shaped something like an exaggerated bread-knife. It is little wonder that that woof will hold water, or stand the trampling of a lifetime. Every thread of it is rammed home with a series of vicious jabs sufficient to make it "set down and stay sot." For each unit of the frequently intricate pattern she has a separate skein; and the unhesitating skill with which she brings them in at their proper intervals is astonishing.

Now, by the time her woof has risen to a point twenty-five to thirty inches above the ground, it is evident that some new arrangement is essential to her convenience. Does she get up and stand to the job? Not at all. She simply loosens the spirally wound rope on the pole above so that its loops hang a foot or two lower, thus letting down the supplementary yarn-beam and the yarn-beam by the same amount. She then makes a fold in the loosened web, and tightly sews the upper edge of this fold to the cloth-beam below, thus making the web taut again. This is the Navajo patent for overcoming the lack of our "revolving cloth-bearers." This operation is repeated several times before a full-sized blanket is completed. The smallest size of saddle blanket can be woven without changing the loom at all.

All Navajo blankets are single ply, the pattern being the

same on both sides. I have seen but two which had on one side a different pattern from that on the other.

The range of quality in Navajo blankets is great. The common blanket, for bedding and rough wear, is a rude thing indeed beside its feast-day brother. These cheap ones, almost always of full size — about six by five feet — are made of the native wool. The Navajos raise their own sheep, shear them, card, twist, and dye the wool. The prevailing color of the blanket is natural — a whitish gray — and through this ground run cross-stripes, generally of blue, but sometimes of red, black, or yellow. These stripes are mostly in native dyes, the blue being now obtained from American indigo. They also dye in any color with dyes made by themselves from herbs and minerals. These wool blankets require a week or so for weaving, and sell at from two dollars and a half to eight dollars apiece. They are frequently half an inch thick, and are the warmest of blankets, their fuzzy softness making them much warmer than the higher-priced, tighter-woven, and consequently stiffer ones.

In the second grade of blankets there is an almost endless variety. These are now made of Germantown yarn, which the Navajos buy in big skeins at the various stores and trad-ing-posts along the line of the Atlantic and Pacific Railway, which passes some twenty-five miles south of the whole line of their reservation. And remarkably fine blankets they make of it. Their ability as inventors of neat designs is truly remarkable. The cheap blankets are very much of a piece; but when you come up into patterns, it would be

difficult to find in the whole territory two blankets exactly
alike. The designs are ingenious, characteristic, and admira-
bly worked out. Sometimes the weaver traces the pattern on
the sand before beginning her blanket, but as a rule she
composes it in her head as the work progresses. Circles or
curved lines are never used in these blankets. The prevailing patterns are straight stripes, diagonals, regular zigzags,
diamonds and crosses—the latter being to the Indians em-
blems of the morning or evening star.

The colors used are limited in number. Scarlet is the
favorite red, and indigo almost the only blue in use. These
and the white of the bleached wool are the original colors,
and the only ones which appear in the very best blankets.
It is curious that these savages should have chosen our own
"red, white, and blue" long before we did—they were weaving already before the first European ever saw America. The
Spanish conquerors brought the first sheep to the New World,
and soon gave these valuable animals to the Pueblo Indians.
So wool came into New Mexico and displaced the Indian cotton, and the Navajos quickly adopted the new material.

But of late there has been a sad deterioration in Navajo
weaving—the Indians have learned one of the mean lessons
of civilization, and now make their blankets less to wear
than to sell. So an abominable combination of colors has
crept in, until it is very difficult longer to get a blanket with
only the real Indian hues. Black, green, and yellow are
sometimes found in superb blankets, and so combined as not
to lessen their value; but as a rule these colors are to be

avoided. But now some weavers use colors which to an Indian are actually accursed—like violet, purple, dark brown, etc., the colors of witchcraft—and such blankets are worthless to collectors. With any Indian, color is a matter of religion, and red is the most sacred of hues. The amount of it in a blanket largely determines the price. An amusing instance of the Navajo devotion to red was brought to my notice some years ago. A post trader had received a shipment of prepared coffee, half in red papers and half in blue. In a month every red package was gone, and every blue package was left on the shelves; nor would the Indians accept the blue even then until long waiting convinced them that there was no present prospect of getting any more red.

The largest of these Germantown-yarn blankets take several weeks to weave, and are worth from fifteen to fifty dollars.

The very highest grade of Navajo blanket is now very rare. It is a dozen years since one of them has been made; the yarn blankets, which are far less expensive and sell just as well to the ignorant traveler, have entirely supplanted them. Only a few of the precious old ones remain—a few in the hands of wealthy Pueblo Indians and Mexicans—and they are almost priceless. I know every such blanket in the southwest, and, outside of one or two private collections, the specimens can be counted on one's fingers. The colors of these choicest blankets are red, white, and blue, or, rarely, just red and white. In a very few specimens there is also a little black. Red is very much the prevailing color, and takes up sometimes four-fifths of the blanket, the other colors merely drawing the pattern on a red ground.

This red material is from a fine Turkish woolen cloth, called *balleta*. It used to be imported to Mexico, whence the Navajos procured it at first. Later, it was sold at some of the trading-posts in this territory. The fixed price of it was six dollars a pound. The Navajos used to ravel this cloth and use the thread for their finest blankets; and it made such blankets as never have been produced elsewhere. Their durability is wonderful. They never fade, no matter how frequently washed — an operation in which *amole*, the saponaceous root of the *palmilla*, should be substituted for soap. As for wear, I have seen balleta blankets which have been used for rugs on the floors of populous Mexican houses for fifty years, which still retain their brilliant color, and show serious wear only at their broken edges. And they will hold water as well as canvas will.

A balleta blanket like that shown in the frontispiece is worth two hundred dollars, and not a dozen of them could be bought at any price. It is seventy-three inches long by fifty-six inches wide, and weighs six pounds. You can easily reckon that the thread in it cost something, at six dollars a pound, and the weaving occupied a Navajo woman for many months. It is hardly thicker than the cover of this book, and is almost as firm. It is too thin and stiff to be an ideal bed-blanket, and it was never meant to be one. All blankets of that quality were made to be worn upon the shoulders of chiefs; and most of them were *ponchos* — that is, they

18

had a small slit left in the center for the wearer to put his head through, so that the blanket would hang upon him like a cape. Thus it was combined overcoat, waterproof, and adornment. I bought this specimen, after weeks of diplomacy, from Martin del Valle, the noble-faced old Indian who has been many times governor of the cliff-built "city" of Acoma. He bought it twenty years ago from a Navajo war-chief for a lot of ponies and turquoise. He has used it ever since, but it is as brilliant, and apparently as strong, as the day it was finished.

These finest blankets are seldom used or shown except upon festal occasions, such as councils, dances, and races. They are then brought forth with all the silver and beaded buckskin, and in a large crowd of Indians make a truly startling display. Some wear them the middle girt around the waist by a belt of heavy silver disks, the lower end falling below the knees, the upper end thrown loosely over the shoulders. Others have them thrown across the saddle, and others tie them in an ostentatious roll behind.

The Navajos and Pueblos also weave remarkably fine and beautiful belts and garters, from two to eight inches wide and two to nine feet long; and durable and pretty dresses for their women.

The loom for weaving one of the handsome belts worn by Pueblo women is quite as simple as that of the Navajos for weaving blankets. One end of the warp is fastened to a stake driven into the ground in front of the weaver, the other to a rod held in place by a strap around her waist; so to tighten the warp she has only to sit back a little. The device for separating the alternate threads of the warp so that the shuttle can be pushed through looks like a small rolling-pin; and in the weaver's right hand is the oak batten-stick for ramming the threads of the woof tightly together. The weaver sits flat upon the ground; generally upon a blanket to keep her *manta* clean, for the dress of a Pueblo woman is neat, handsome, and expensive. These belts are always two-ply, that is, the pattern on one side is different from that on the other.

It may also be news to you to learn that both Navajos and Pueblos are admirable silversmiths, and make all their own jewelry. Their silver rings, bracelets, earrings, buttons, belts, dress pins, and bridle ornaments are very well fashioned with a few rude tools. The Navajo smith works on a flat stone under a tree; but the Pueblo artificer has generally a bench and a little forge in a room of his house.

XVI.

THE BLIND HUNTERS.

N these Strange Corners a great many things seem to be exactly reversed from what we are accustomed to. For instance, with us "a hunter's eye" is a synonym for perfect sight, and we fancy that if any one in the world needs good vision it is he who follows the chase. But in the quaint southwest the most important hunters—and, in the belief of thousands of the natives, the most successful ones—cannot see at all! They are stone-blind, which is not so out of keeping, after all, since they themselves are stones! Very pretty stones are these famous little Nimrods—snowy quartz, or brilliant agate, or jasper, or a peculiar striped spar which is found in some parts of New Mexico. That is their body. Then their eyes are of coral, or blue turquoise from the prehistoric mines in Mount Chalchuhuitl near Santa Fé; and their hearts are always of turquoise, which is the most precious thing known to the aborigines of the southwest, for it is the stone which stole its color from the sky.

"But how can a blind stone with a turquoise heart be a hunter?" you ask. Well, that depends on the locality. I do not imagine he would count for much in a Queen's County fox-chase, but out here he can be a hunter very well. Here he is the very king of hunters; and no party of Indians would think for an instant of going out for deer or antelope, or even rabbits, except under his leadership and with his aid.

These stone hunters are the hunt-fetiches of the Indians. They are tiny images of the most successful animals of prey— like the cougar, bear, eagle, and wolf—rudely carved from the hardest stone into a clumsy but unmistakable likeness. The image alone is not enough. An arrow-head of agate or volcanic glass is always bound with sinew to its right side, and under the turquoise heart is always a pinch of the sacred corn-meal. These little stone statues are supposed to communicate to those who carry them all the hunter-craft of the animal which they represent. Every Indian carries a fetich when he hunts, and derives its power from it by putting its mouth to his own and drawing in his breath—"drinking the breath" of the image. This ceremony is indispensable at the beginning of a hunt, and at various stages of its progress. The favorite hunt-fetich among the Pueblos is the mountain-lion or cougar, *keem-ée-deh*, which they deem the king of animals.

The hunter, when he strikes a trail, takes a forked twig and places it in front of a footprint, with the fork opening backward. This is to trip the fleeing game. Then he draws from his "left-hand bag" (the shoulder-pouch which serves the Indian for a pocket) his fetich, inhales its "breath of strength," and prays to it—or rather to the animal spirit it represents

—to help him ; and then, before following the trail, imitates
the roar of his patron-beast, to terrify and bewilder the game.
He firmly believes that without these superstitious ceremonials he would stand no chance at all in the hunt, but that
with them he is sure to succeed.

It is difficult for us to realize the importance which the
Indian attaches to all matters connected with game. We are
at a point in civilization where such things concern us only
as pastimes, but to the Indian the hunt is still the corner-
stone of life, or has been until so recently that he has not
lost the old feeling. A matter so vital to the human race—
in his eyes—has become the nucleus for a vast quantity of
his most sacred beliefs. The animals which are successful
hunters are objects of reverence, and he is careful to invoke
their aid, that his own pursuit may be as fortunate as theirs.
Indeed, the whole process of hunting is involved in an enormous amount of religious "red-tape"—for you must remember that the Indian never does *anything* simply "for fun."
He enjoys many things ; but he does them not for enjoyment,
but for a superstitious end.

Even my neighbors, the Pueblos, who have been farmers
and irrigators for unknown centuries, preserve almost un-
abated their ancient traditions and usages of the chase, and
a hunt of any sort is a very religious affair, whether it be a
simple foray of two or three men, or one of the great communal hunts in which many hundreds are engaged. One of
their chief branches of medicine-men are those who have absolute control of all matters pertaining to game. These are

named, in the language of the Tigua Pueblos, the *Hóo-mah-koon* (" those who have death in their arms "). According to their folk-lore the Hóo-mah-koon were created just after mankind emerged from the bowels of the earth, and were the first of all branches of medicine, except only the *Káh-pee-oo-nin* (" those who are dying of cold," in allusion to the almost nakedness in which they always make their official appearance), who broke through the crust of the earth and led their people out to the light.

In the sacred songs of the Hóo-mah-koon of the Pueblo of Isleta, where I lived for four years, it is declared that they came here first from the town of the Wolf's Den, one of the picturesque ruins in the great plains east of the Manzano Mountains. The order in Isleta numbers seven men. Beginning in May of every year there is always a series of communal rabbit hunts, one a week for seven weeks. The first of these hunts is under the command of the senior Hóo-mah-koo-ée-deh (the singular of Hóo-mah-koon), the second hunt under the next in rank, and so on until each of the captains of the hunt has had a day in the order of his seniority.

The official crier of the village announces the night before that on the morrow will be *Nah-kú-ah-shú* (the round-hunt), in stentorian tones which none but the deaf can fail to hear. That evening the Hóo-mah-koon and other dignitaries hold *Náh-wheh* (the drawing-dance), to charm the game. The dancing and singing are supposed (though conducted in a house) to reach and fascinate the ears of all wild animals, so that they cannot hear the approach of the hunter on the morrow; and in the intervals of the dance all who are present smoke vigorously the *weer*, or sacred cigarette, whose clouds blind the eyes of the game and make them less watchful. The songs sung at the drawing-dance vary according to the game to be hunted next day, and always begin with a refrain that has no meaning, but is an imitation of the cry of that animal. Before the great fall round-hunt for deer and antelope, the song is one which may be translated as follows:

HUNTING SONG.

Beh-eh eh-k'hay-roh,
Beh-eh eh-k'hay-roh,
Beh-eh eh-k'hay-roh.
I am the mountain-lion young man,
I am the mountain-lion young man,
I am the mountain-lion young man,
Antelope thigh in my house hangs plenty,
Antelope shoulder in my house hangs plenty,
Antelope heart in my house hangs plenty,
I am the mountain-lion young man,
Deer head in my house hangs plenty,
Deer liver in my house hangs plenty,
All deer meat in my house hangs plenty,
I am the mountain-lion young man.

The dance and other services last most of the night. At the appointed time in the morning the Hóo-mah-koon repair to a certain sand-hill on the edge of the plains, about two miles from the pueblo, the invariable starting-point for all hunts to the westward, and thither follow several hundred of the men and grown boys of the village. At a certain sacred spot the chief of the Hóo-mah-koon starts a small fire with the most impressive ceremonies, singing meanwhile a chant

which relates how fire was first discovered and how transmit-
ted—both of which important deeds are credited to the Hóo-
mah-koon. None outside that order—not even a member
of one of the other branches of medicine-men—dare make
that fire, and the chief Hóo-mah-koo-ée-deh must light it
only in the sacred way, namely, with the ancient fire-drill or
with flint and steel. He would expect to be struck dead if
he were to kindle it with the impious, new-fangled matches,
which are now used by the Pueblos for all common uses, but
must not enter any sacred ceremony whatever.

When the holy fire is well under way the Hóo-mah-koon
stand around it with bowed heads, invoke the fetiches, and
pray to Those Above to bless the hunt. Then their chief
selects two men to lead the hunt, puts them in front of
all the crowd, instructs them where to close the circle, and
pushes them apart with the command "Go!" These two
start running in divergent lines. In a moment two more
are started after them, and two more, and so on until all the
hundreds of hunters are in motion along two files like the
arms of a V, the knot of Hóo-mah-koon forming the apex.
The two leaders run on for a designated distance, all the time
getting farther apart, and then begin to converge toward one
another until they meet at the appointed spot, frequently a
couple of miles from the starting-point. Meeting, they hold
their clubs in the right hand, pass each other on the same
side and make cross-lines on the ground, by which they stand.

By this time a cordon of hunters in the shape of an ellipse
has been formed by their followers, and now at the signal

from the Hóo-mah-koon the cordon begins to shrink inward, the old men smoking continually to keep the game blinded. The hunters are armed only with boomerangs, which they hurl with force and precision that are simply marvelous. Very little game that has been surrounded thus ever escapes, even to the swift-winged quail. A dozen or more of these big surrounds are made in the course of the day, and all the game that is killed in the first two goes to the Hóo-mah-koo-ée-deh who is in command for that day. The Hóo-mah-koon get their peculiar name from the fact that as soon as an animal is killed they sit down and hug it upon their laps, sprinkling it with the sacred meal.

In the evening, when the successful hunters return to the pueblo, heavily laden with game, they proceed to the house of the cacique (the chief religious official) and sing before it the following song, unchanged from the days when they hunted the lordliest game on the American continent:

SONG AFTER THE HUNT.

Ah, ee-yah, ee-yah, hay h'yah-ee-ah,
Ah, ee-yah, ee-yah, hay h'yah-ee-ah,
Ah, ee-yah, ee-yah, hay h'yah-ee-ah.
Yonder in the wee-ow-weew-bahn,
       [In Indian Territory]
There stays the buffalo,
Commander of beasts,
Him we are driving
Hither from yonder,
With him as prey
We are arriving,
With him as prey
Now we come in.

As the last line is sung, some of the hunters enter the house of the cacique, bearing a present of game.

His own share each hunter carries to his home, and when the animal is cooked its head is invariably given to him who kills it. By eating this the hunter is supposed to acquire something from the animal itself which will make him successful in killing others of its kind. The Pueblos have a curious custom concerning rabbits, which are now more numerous than any other game, hundreds being killed in every round-hunt on the plain. They will not, under any circumstances, fry them, nor touch one which has been thus cooked. The only way in which a True Believer will prepare rabbit is to "make it as people." The animal is skinned and drawn. Then its long ears are twisted into a knot on top of its head; the fore-legs are twisted so that their ankles are under the "arm-pits," and the hind legs are crossed and pinned behind the back. Why this extraordinary distortion should be deemed to make poor bunny look "like people," I have never been able to learn; nor yet the cause for this custom, except that it was given them "by those of old," and that the Trues order it to be continued. After it has been trussed up in this shape the rabbit is roasted in one of the quaint adobe out-door ovens, or stewed whole in a big earthen jar with home-ground corn-meal.

No private party ever thinks of starting on a hunting trip without first securing the intercession of the Hóo-mah-koon with Those Above for their success and safety. When a number of men decide to go on a hunt, or on any other jour-

ney, they meet and select the wisest among them to go to
the Hóo-mah-koon and ask them to "give the road." The ambassador chosen for this important and honorable mission
at once bids his wife, mother, or sister to prepare the sacred
meal, without which no such request would dare be made of
the medicine-men. She selects and grinds the white or yellow corn to meal, and wraps it in the ceremonial corn-husk
wrapper; and the ambassador thus equipped goes with his
request to the chief Hóo-mah-koo-ée-deh. The medicine-man
takes the sacred meal with his right hand and holds it all the
time the ambassador is present, and names the night when
he will come to a designated house (that of one of the party),
foretell the fortunes of their journey, and "give the road."

After eight o'clock on the appointed night, which is almost
invariably the one before the hunters are to start, all the
Hóo-mah-koon gather at that house, where the hunters are
present with such of their friends as desire to be benefited.
The Hóo-mah-koon go through the usual jugglery of a medicine-dance, and then proceed to forecast the proposed journey, taking their omens in any number of ways, somewhat
after the fashion of the soothsayers of ancient Greece and
Rome. In one case in my knowledge a prominent Indian
here was going to travel horseback several hundred miles to
trade with the Mescalero Apaches. The chief Hóo-mah-koo-
ée-deh went out and combed the horse that was to be ridden,
and returned with the combings, which he began to sort over
with great solemnity. At last he handed to the traveler a
lot of light hairs with one dark one among them, and said:

"You are on your way to break the rifle you carry, for the horse will fall and throw you as you go down a hill. And you will trade the broken rifle for this dark horse," pointing to the one dark hair. The traveler, who is a very reliable Indian, and who made one of the best governors the pueblo ever had, vows that it befell exactly so. His horse threw him, the rifle was broken in the fall, and he traded it for a horse the very color of that hair! Who could ask more convincing proof that the medicine-man had indeed "the power"?

After the fortunes of the journey have been thus foretold all present join in the following chant. At the words "Hither! Hither!" those who are to travel draw their hands toward them repeatedly, and the others perform a similar incantation with their breath. This is intended to "draw to" the traveler the game or other object of his journey.

SONG BEFORE THE JOURNEY.

Hither! Hither!
This way! This way!
[Pointing in the direction to be taken.]
Life for-the-sake-of,
Health for-the-sake-of,
Our children for-the-sake-of,
Our animals for-the-sake-of,
Game for-the-sake-of,
Clothing for-the-sake of,
Thus with empty hands
Thus we go out.

As the last two lines are sung all brush their left palms with their right. After this song the Hóo-mah-koon pray to

19

the Trues to bless the journey, and then "give the road"—
that is, their official permission to start.

The Pueblos have, by the way, a "coyote telegraph," which
is used in hunts, and used to be in war, by which they can
impart news or commands several miles by yells which are a
perfect imitation of the coyote Any one who had not learned
the "code" would imagine it merely the usual concert of the
cowardly little wolves of the prairie.   The cry of the genuine
coyote, too, is always a significant omen to the Pueblo.   One
short, sharp bark is a token of impending danger, and any
party that hears that warning will at once turn back, no
matter how important its mission.   Two short cries close together mean that some one is dead in the village.   Three
short successive yelps, followed by the long wail, is understood as sure proof that the principals of the town have tried
some person accused of witchcraft and have found a verdict
of guilty ; and so on.

XVII.

MONG the countless oddities of custom which prevail in the southwest, perhaps none would strike my young countrymen as odder than the graduating exercises of a Pueblo lad. It is certainly a very different sort of graduation from any known to eastern schools; and I fear a great many of our bright pupils would fail to pass to the satisfaction of the examiners.

Among all Indian tribes there is a much more thorough course of home education than we generally imagine. Any observant man, if he be half as intelligent as the average Indian, cannot watch the latter without feeling that this brown fellow has a remarkable scholarship of the senses. The education of eye and ear, and of the perceptive faculties, is nothing short of marvelous to us, who have not left of any of these senses a tithe of the acuteness Nature meant us to have. But if the observer can get "on the inside of things" and really understand Indian life, he finds a much more remarkable education in the strange lore of a strange people.

Such memories are hardly ever found among "civilized" people as are common to those who have no books nor writing to *remember for them;* and it takes such marvelous memories to retain all that the member of Indian society must carry in his head. I have found the study of the training of my young Pueblo neighbors very interesting.

The girls are taught little beyond their duties as home-makers and home-keepers—which is a considerable education in itself, for the Pueblo woman is a very good housewife. But the boys all go through a very serious and arduous training to fit them for the responsibilities of Indian manhood. Every lad is expected to become an athlete of agility and endurance, to be expert in war and the hunt, to know and keep word for word the endless stories which embody the customs and laws of his people, and to be educated in many other ways. His training begins as soon as he can talk and be talked to; and it continues, in greater or less degree, as long as he lives. As for the lad who is elected to follow the unattractive life of a medicine-man, he has before him one long curriculum of toil. In all Indian tribes the shamans or medicine-men are the most important personages—the real "power behind the throne," no matter what the outward form of government. Upon them depends the success of the farmer, the hunter, the warrior; they have to keep witches from swooping off the people, to give proper welcome to new-comers to this world, to cure the sick, and give safeguard to the departed on their long journey to the Other Country. Besides the extremely numerous societies of medicine-men, there are many other secret orders among the Pueblos; and initiation into one or more of these is part of the education of the young Indian boy.

Some time ago a bright young neighbor and friend of mine, then twelve years old, was received into the important order of the Cum-pa-huít-la-wen — who are a sort of police against witches and armed guards of the Fathers of Medicine. In his infancy Refugio had been sickly, and to induce the Trues to spare his life his parents had "given" him to the gray-headed chief of the Cum-pa-huít-la-wen. This old shaman thus became Refugio's "medicine-father," and used to visit him regularly—for the boy continued to live with his real parents. This giving for adoption into an order or into another clan is common among the Pueblos. It does not at all break up the home ties, but merely gives the boy an extra godfather as it were. The first day after the adoption, the old shaman came in person, inquired as to the boy's health, held him awhile in his arms, prayed for him, and went away. Next day the second in authority of the Cum-pa-huít-la-wen called and did likewise; the third day, the third in rank; and so on until every member of the order had made his ceremonial visit. Then the chief shaman began again, and after him day by day came his medicine-brothers in the order of their rank. These formal visits had been kept up daily, through all these years, with absolute punctuality, until Refugio was deemed old enough to become a full member of the lodge into which he had been adopted. All this time, of course, he had been under the general tuition of the order;

and his "brothers" had given him a general education—but had not intrusted him with their special secrets.

When at last his initiation was decided upon, he was made to keep a solemn fast for twenty-four hours. Then, after undown, he was led by his medicine-father to the medicine-house, where the whole order of Cum-pa-huít-la-wen were already assembled.

Removing their moccasins at the door, the old chief and the lad entered the low, dark room—lighted only by the sacred fire, whose flickering embers flung ghostly shadows across the dark rafters—and stood before the solemn semicircle of squatting men. Standing there with bowed head, the medicine-father prayed to the Trues of the East, the Trues of the North, the Trues of the West, the Trues of the South, the Trues Above and the Trues Here-in-the-Center. So punctilious is Pueblo superstition that it would be deemed an infamy to address their six cardinal points in any other order. Only a witch would ever think of naming first North, then West, South, etc. Having thus invoked the blessing of all the deities, the old man took the trembling lad by the hand and said to his fellows: "Brothers, friends, this is my son. From now, he is to take our road. Receive him and teach him in the ways of the Cum-pa-huít-la-wen."

"It is well," replied the others. "*Ah-hlai!* Sit down on what ye have."

The old man and Refugio placed their moccasins and shoulder-blankets upon the bare adobe floor, and seated

themselves thereon.   It would be an unheard-of sacrilege for
an Indian to occupy a chair or bench upon any such sacred
occasion.   He must sit only "upon what he has"—and if it
be summer, when no blanket is worn, his moccasins are his
only seat.

Then the chief shaman's first assistant—had the boy been
adopted by any of the others, the chief himself would have
officiated now—prepared and handed them the *weer*, or
sacred cigarette.   The ordinary cigarette of tobacco rolled
in a bit of corn-husk or brown paper, which is commonly
smoked for pleasure, is never used in a religious ceremony.
The *weer* can be lighted only at the sacred fire ; and having
kindled his at the coals, Refugio began to puff slowly, as he
had been directed.   This smoke-trying is always the first duty
of a candidate, and it is no mean test of the earnestness of his
desire to "take the road."   He must smoke the *weer* down to
its last whiff and inhale every particle of smoke, not a suspicion of which must escape from his mouth.   The first three
or four whiffs almost invariably make him deathly sick, but
it is very rarely indeed that he fails to smoke to the end.   In
almost all folk-stories wherein the hero goes into the presence of the Trues for any assistance—a very common part
of the plot of these myths—he is tried with the *weer* first, to
see if he be enough of a man for it to be worth the while
of the Trues to attend to his case.   Sometimes the trial of
his faith is long-drawn and harrowing in its severity, but
it always begins with the smoke test.

Refugio did bravely. Very soon the soft olive of his young face turned gray; but he puffed away impassively at the pungent reed until he had finished the last whiff.

"*Ah-t'it-mée-hee!* He wins his course!" said the first assistant shaman. Then, with prayers by all, the cleansing with warm water was given Refugio, and he was bidden to stand erect, while the master of ceremonies said encouragingly: "So far, you show that you will follow our road."

Standing, now, the lad was ordered to make a prayer to all the Trues—no small task, since their number is legion and they must be addressed only in the proper order of their rank. Whenever Refugio stumbled or was at a loss, the first assistant prompted him; and he had to go over and over that enormous list until he knew it perfectly.

Now he was made to sit down upon his moccasins, with his knees drawn up under his chin, to learn the songs of the order—which are of great number. He began with the great song to T'hoo-rée-deh, the Sun-Father—which he learned in less than half the time it afterward took me to master it. It is a very important and impressive song, and is sung by the Cum-pa-huít-la-wen whenever they escort the cacique to a great ceremony. A translation of it is as follows (leaving out the many repetitions and meaningless refrains):

THE SONG OF THE SUN.

O Sun, our Father,
Sun-Man,
Sun-Commander,
Father, a prayer-stick we tie.

Father, on the road stand ready;
Father, take your way;
Father, arrive;
Father, come in;
Father, be seated.

The learning of all those songs was a serious matter, and
Refugio mastered only a few that night. The next day at
sundown—after another fast—he resumed his labors, and
so on every night until he had all the songs by heart. After
the last one was learned came the ceremony of *Tho-a-shúr*, the
Receiving. The boy stood with bowed head in the center of
the room, while the master of ceremonies gave him the ceremonial embrace—putting his right arm over Refugio's left
shoulder, and his left arm under Refugio's right—and prayed
that all the Trues would bless the new Cum-pa-huit-la-wíd-
deh. Then Refugio was embraced in turn by his medicine-
father and all the other members, and was given to drink of
P'ah-cuín-p'ah, the Sacred Water—a secret mixture which
has a sweet smell but no taste.

Now came the last severe test of Refugio's faith. He was
seated, no longer in front of, but in, the semicircle of Cum-
pa-huít-la-wen, who sat solemnly with their official bows and
arrows in their hands. For all secular purposes the Indians
now use the latest and best fire-arms; but only bows and
arrows can be admitted to religious ceremonials. The oldest
member of the lodge began to recite the history and customs
of the Cum-pa-huít-la-wen, from the very beginning, when
mankind came out from the Black Lake of Tears, down to
the present day. For *forty-nine hours* this recital was con-

tinued without rest, the elder shamans taking turns in telling; and all that weary time the boy had to keep awake and intent, answering at the proper points " *Tab-kóon-nam*—is that so ? " Once, when he nodded, the nearest man gave him a sharp punch in the ribs with the end of his bow.

When Refugio had passed this last ordeal with credit, he was again embraced, and the official announcement was made that he was now a full Cum-pa-huít-la-wíd-deh. Had he failed in any of these tests—so hard upon the endurance of a young boy—he would have been told to "take the heart of a man" (be brave) and try again; and the second trial would have been given him in a few days. The neophyte's struggles with his sickness and sleepiness are sometimes very comical; but the men never smile at him—indeed, their treatment of him is invariably very kind, as is their conduct toward children under all circumstances.

Refugio was now technically "finished" or graduated, but his tasks were by no means done. He has before him a lifetime of hard and patient study, infinite practice, and frequent self-denial. To acquire that marvelous legerdemain which gives the medicine-men their chief prestige is a matter of years of persevering practice. He will have, too, to go through innumerable fasts—some of them for as long as eight days—and many other mortifications of the flesh. The life of a medicine-man is as far as possible from an easy one. The responsibility for the welfare of the whole pueblo—here nearly twelve hundred souls—rests upon his shoulders; and at the cost of his own comfort and health he must secure blessings for his people and avert all ill from them. His rewards are very few, and entirely disproportionate, except the universal respect which he commands.

Refugio, by the way, has now earned the proud privilege of smoking. He often comes to me for the wherewithal to roll the little brown cigarettes of the country in his slender fingers. How rare a privilege this is for so young a boy, under the rigid Pueblo etiquette, you will understand better when I have told you something about their notions on the subject of smoking.

XVIII.

THE PRAYING SMOKE.

HE use of the pipe of peace by the Indians of the East, who have disappeared before the elbowing of our ancestors the earth-hungry, is familiar to every reader; but few are aware how widespread is still the importance of smoking among the surviving tribes of the continent. In the southwest, where the Indian has held his own since the more merciful Spanish conquest—for the real history of later days proves that the Spaniards were not the merciless brutes they were so long termed—the calumet had never any real place, though a few stone pipes have been found here. The cigarette is the official form of the weed, and its importance is surprising. In religion, in war, in the chase, and in society it occupies a highly responsible position. It is more to the Indian than is salt to the Arab—equal as a hospitable bond, and extending to countless other uses to which the Arabian salt is never promoted.

I should not wish to be understood as saying these things of the abominable little white cylinders familiar to the East. Neither Indian nor Mexican has quite fallen to those. The *cigarro* of the southwest is not a pestilence. Its component parts are a pinch of granulated tobacco, a bit of sweet-corn husk, or (specially made) brown paper and a twist of the wrist.

In my studies in New Mexico I have been much interested in the sacred smoke. It recurs everywhere. There is hardly a folk-story among the Pueblo Indians in which it does not figure prominently. Not a prayer is offered nor a ceremonial conducted without its aid. But for it the land would be burned up with drought, and the population harpied away bodily by evil spirits. No one thinks of being born or dying without the intervention of the cigarette, and to all the intermediate phases of life it is equally indispensable. And as befits so vital an article of faith, it is surrounded by rigid restrictions. Thus much is common also to the Mexican population. A Mexican boy would as soon think of putting his head in the fire as of smoking before his parents, if he dared smoke at all — which is very seldom. Many a time on a weary march I have offered the bit of corn-husk and the pinch of tobacco to an old man, who accepted gratefully, and another to his grown-up son, who politely but firmly declined, though I could see he was dying for a smoke; and he would deny himself till night, when he could sneak off up the cañon with the precious luxuries and grunt with joy as he puffed away in loneliness and gloom. And many a time I have seen a full-grown man, with mature children of his own, burn his fingers in hastily pinching out his cigarette at the unexpected approach of his aged father or mother. Mexican women

20

may smoke after their marriage, but of course with the same restriction.

With the Indians the lines are more closely drawn. A woman is not to think of smoking. I have known a case where an Indian girl, who had learned this and other bad habits from the superior race, was caught by her parents with a cigarette in her mouth; and her tongue was slit at the tip as a warning against such unladylike tricks. The Pueblo lad dare not smoke even by himself before he is twenty-five years old, unless he has established his warlike prowess by taking a scalp,* or has been given "the freedom of the smoke" upon acquiring full membership in one of the branches of medicine-men, like Refugio. And even then he must not smoke in presence of his parents or any one who is his senior, without their direct permission, which is very seldom given.

In all Pueblo dealings with their brethren and other Indians the cigarette is a flag of truce, a covenant, a bond whose sanctity was never violated. When a Pueblo meets any heathen Indian—for all Pueblos rank themselves as Christians—his first act is to toss him the little *guaje* of tobacco with a corn-husk. He never hands it. If the stranger pick up the offering, there is unbreakable peace between them, and they sit down and smoke the sacred smoke in amity, though their respective people may be at war. If an Indian went out to slay his bitterest foe and

---

* Of course it is now a great while since they have earned the privilege thus.

in a thoughtless moment accepted a cigarette from him, he would have to forego the coveted scalp.

It is only recently that I have been able to settle the mooted question whether the Indians of the southwest smoked before the Spaniards came, three hundred and fifty years ago, for these Indians did not have tobacco until after the conquest. This late but conclusive evidence establishes the fact that they did smoke. The ancient substitutes for tobacco were two herbs known in Tigua as *ku-a-rée* and *p'ee-én-hleh*. They are much more aromatic than tobacco, but do not, as the Indians observe, "make drunk so much" as our weed. I have been unable to get green specimens of the plants for classification. The dried leaves are brought great distances from certain spots in the mountains.

In the primitive cigarette, which the Tiguans call *weer*, no paper was used, of course, for this country was then innocent of paper; nor were corn-husks. The *weer* was made by punching out the pith of a reed common in the Rio Grande valley, and ramming the hollow full of p'ee-én-hleh or ku-a-rée. All ceremonial cigarettes are so made still; for the brown paper or *oja* smoke is "not good" for religious matters. The reed, however, may be filled with tobacco instead of the older weeds and still be efficacious.

Himself an altogether matchless observer, the Indian is equally adept at eluding observation. If he has a secret duty to perform when you are around, he will do it before your very face with such *sang-froid* and such wizardly sleight of hand that you will never dream what he is doing, or that he is doing anything out of the ordinary. I had watched the sacred-smoke prayer ten thousand times without the remotest suspicion of it, and my observation was neither indifferent nor without the sharpening which association with Indians must give the dullest senses. It was only after a hint, and when I came one day to see—myself unseen—an old Indian lighting his cigarette, and noticed that each of the first six puffs was sent in a different direction, that I began to suspect a ceremony and to watch for further proof. Then I saw that every smoker did the same thing, though, when in company, with an infinite precaution which made it almost imperceptible. The world is full of evil spirits—nothing else is so ever-present in the Indian mind as the fear of witches—and these must be propitiated as well as the Trues. This cardinal smoking at the outset of the cigarette is both an offering to the Trues and exorcism of witches.

It is the collective smoke of the sacred *weer* that forms the rain-clouds and brings the rain. Tobacco smoke has not this virtue. In the spring medicine-making, when the year is to be foretold, and at any special medicine-making that may be had to stave off a threatened drought, the whole *junta* industriously smokes *weer*, to help with its cloud-compelling vapor in the answer of their own prayers for rain. Since in the preparation for one of these ceremonials the medicine-men have to shut themselves up in the medicine-house for from four to eight days—never going out, nor eating, nor moving from their appointed seats, and with no relief save drinking water and smoking—their united efforts in that time make a cloud surely sufficient in volume, whatever may be its capacities for precipitation.

I have already told you of the "drawing-dance" before every hunt, wherein the *weer* is smoked to blind the eyes of the game; and that in the hunt itself a steady smoking is kept up by the shamans of the chase for the same purpose. The *weer* also figures in *all* medicine-makings, to dispel witches and for other purposes. In looking into the magic *cajete*, the Father of All Medicine stoops and blows the sacred smoke slowly across the water in that important bowl, and it is *then* that he can see in that curious mirror (so he says) all that is going on in the world. The manner in which the film of vapor hovers upon the water or curls up from it in hasty spirals indicates whether the year will be calm or windy. This smoke mirror is also particularly used in the detection of witches, whom it reveals in their evil tricks, however hidden.

When one is sick the male head of the family wraps a few pinches of tobacco in a corn-husk, ties the packet with a corn-husk string, and with this offering goes to the medicine-man and requests him to come and cure the invalid. And it is a sovereign fee — a shaman whose services you cannot hire by whatsoever present of money or valuables cannot refuse your request if you come to him with an offering of the weed. This certainly indicates a freedom from avarice which the professional men of more civilized races do not always imitate, for the Indian is as fond of his family as are any of us, and would pay his last pony and last silver necklace for the

curing of his sick if it were demanded. Indeed, the whole
shaman code of ethics is a very creditable one.

The ceremonial *weer* dare not be lighted with a match or
at a common blaze. It can be ignited only from the sacred
fire in the estufa, a coal from the cacique's house, a flint and
steel, or the ancient fire-drill, which is here a dry, round stick
fitting tightly into a cavity in the end of another, and re-
volved rapidly from right to left (even in so trivial a matter
as this the wrong order must be avoided) until the hollow is
sufficiently hot to ignite the primitive tinder under a coaxing
breath. Very old men who are True Believers still dislike
to light even their pleasure cigarettes in the suspicious modern ways, and will, if possible, pluck a coal in their skinny
fingers to start the precious smoke.

When a person dies here, the medicine-men, who come to
insure the safety of the departed on his four days' journey to
the other world, perform very intricate and mysterious rites,
very largely designed to hide his trail from the evil spirits,
who would otherwise be sure to follow and harass him, and
would very likely succeed in switching him off altogether
from the happy land and into "the place where devils are."
Among other things the body is surrounded during these
four days with the tracks of the road-runner * to lead the
witches on a false trail, and the sacred smoke is continuously
blown about that they may not see which way the departed
went.

* A small pheasant.

XIX.

THE DANCE OF THE SACRED BARK.

E would hardly look for refinements of language among Indians, but, like many of our other notions about them, this is not fully correct. They do use euphemisms, and invent pleasant-sounding phrases for unpleasant things. One of the best examples of this is the manner in which they speak of one of their most savage customs. They hardly ever talk of scalps or scalping; instead of those harsh words they have very innocent paraphrases. Among my Tigua neighbors this ghastly trophy is spoken of as "the sacred hair," or "the oak-bark," or "the sacred bark"—all very natural Indian metaphors. An important folk-story of Isleta relates how two boys who smoked before they had proved themselves men were reproved by their grandfather, a wise old medicine-man. He told them that before they could be allowed to smoke they must go to the Eagle Feather Mountains (the Manzano range), and bring him some of the "bark of the oak." The youths went out in all innocence and peeled the bark from several trees, and were greatly chagrined when their grandfather sternly told them to go and try again. At last a wise mole solved the riddle for them, and directed them against a band of marauding Navajos, from whose heads the boys got the "bark" which entitled them thereafter to the privilege of smoking.

It is a good many years since my kindly "friends and fellow-citizens" of the pueblo of Isleta have taken a scalp, and they were never universal snatchers of "the sacred hair." All their traditions assure me that they never did have the habit of scalping Americans, Mexicans, or Pueblo Indians— no Christians, in fact—but only the heathen savages who surrounded them, and for so many bloody centuries harassed and murdered ceaselessly these quiet village people. Moreover, it has always been against their rule to scalp the women of even these barbarous foes.

Some eighteen years must have gone by since the last scalps were brought to Isleta. One of them came at the belt of my pleasant next-door neighbor, Bartolo Jojola. He is one of the official Delight-Makers, or *Kó-sha-re*, and fully competent to hold his own with any civilized clown of the ring. A band of Comanches from over the mountains to the east stole silently into the pueblo one stormy midnight to steal what stock they might. A lot of horses were in a strong corral of palisades, whose tops were bound with iron-like ropes of rawhide. One Comanche climbed quietly into the inclosure, with the end of a lasso in his hand. He at that end, and a companion outside, sawed the rope back and forth until the rawhides were cut. Then several posts were uprooted, the horses were led out, and off went the robbers

and their booty without arousing any one.   But at daybreak
—for my friends are very early risers—the alarm was given.
A posse was organized and followed the robbers across the
Rio Grande, across the twenty-mile plateau east of us, and
over the ten-thousand-foot Manzano Mountains.   At last
they overtook the raiders on the edge of the great plains,
and there was a fierce fight.   The Comanches, who were, as a
tribe, the best horsemen America has ever seen, resorted to
their favorite tactics of savage and repeated cavalry charges.
The Isleteños, though admirable riders, were no match on
horseback for these Centaurs of the plains, so they dis-
mounted and received the charge on foot.   So effective was
the fire of their flint-locks that the Comanches took to flight.
The Isleteños recovered the stolen horses, besides capturing
many new ones and a dozen scalps.

Since then there have been none of these ghastly trophies
brought to Isleta; and yet the scalp plays an important part
in the ceremonials of the village, and in a secret niche in the
wall of the dark, round estufa rests a priceless horde of the
sacred "barks," which are still taken out and danced over at
their due season.

The Indian does not take a scalp through cruelty, but
just as civilized soldiers fight for and preserve the captured
battle-flags of the enemy, as trophies and proofs of prowess
in war.   Not being refined enough to see the barbarity of
taking a physical trophy, he does very much what civilized
nations did not many centuries ago, when ghastly heads on
pikes were no uncommon sight; and he takes it chiefly be-

cause he believes that with it the valor and skill of the former possessor become his own.

The scalp is taken by making a rough circle of slashes around the skull, and then tearing off the broad patch of skin and hair by main force. It is a very dreadful operation, never to be forgotten by those who have once seen it. The trophy must be cured by him who took it, which he proceeds to do with the utmost care. Many magical powers are supposed to reside in the scalp. Even a third party who touches it, by accident or design, becomes possessed of some of its virtues, though he is thereby also forced to certain temporary self-denials.

When a war-party returns to the pueblo with scalps it is a very serious matter. They cannot enter the town, nor can their anxious families come out to meet them. If they have been westward after the Apaches, Navajos, or Utes, they make a solemn halt on the center of the Hill of the Wind, a volcanic peak twelve miles west of here; and if to the east after Comanches, they stop at a corresponding point on their return on the east side of the Rio Grande. There they camp with the scalps, and send one-half their number forward to the pueblo, where they dare not go to their homes, but repair at once to the cacique, and make their report to him. For fourteen days the half who are out on the hills keep their camp, sending out scouts daily to the lookouts in the lava peaks to guard against the approach of an enemy; and the half who have come to town are secluded in the estufa, fasting and forbidden any intercourse with their families. At the end of this two weeks the warriors who have been shut up in the estufa march out and relieve their companions in camp, staying there with the scalps while the others come in to fast in the estufa. After fourteen days more the men in camp start toward town, those from the estufa meet them half-way, and all enter the pueblo singing "man-songs" (songs of war), and carry the scalps first to the cacique and then to the estufa.

Then begins another period of fasting and self-purification —twelve days for those who have touched a scalp in any way, and eight days for those who have not. Every act is regulated with the most minute and scrupulous care. The estufa is always surrounded with the utmost sacredness, and its etiquette is more punctilious than anything we know of. The estufa is a building by itself, round and low, with a diameter of from forty to fifty feet. It has no doors in the sides, but is reached by ladders from ground to roof, and from the roof by another ladder down through a trap-door to the interior. The interior of the estufa is a plain, circular room, with walls bare, save for a few antlers and rude paintings of the sacred animals. One must not forget himself in entering the estufa. Reaching the roof, he must approach the trap-door from the west side, back down the ladder, turn to his right when at the bottom, and make a complete circuit of the room, a foot from the wall, ere he takes his seat in the semicircle around the sacred fire. If he were thoughtlessly to turn to the left in any of these maneuvers, it would be sure death ; for the Trues would let loose on him the ghost of the scalped man, who, clad only in a dark blue breech-clout and with a lasso coiled over his shoulder, would chase and touch him, whereupon he would fall dead! When they come to leave the estufa they approach the foot of the ladder *from* the left, and on reaching the roof turn to the right, walk around the roof, and finally descend to the ground backward, in hard-earned safety.

The seat of the cacique is at the west side of the fireplace; that of his first assistant opposite him on the east, and the acolytes fill the semicircle between. In a semicircle around these are the Cum-pa-huít-la-wen, who are guards of the estufa; and in successive semicircles come all the rest of the audience. All face away from the fire until the cacique rises and speaks, when all face toward it, and so remain through the rest of the session. This sacred fire is made only by the Hóo-mah-koon, and must be started with only the sacred fire-drill or flint and steel. Most of the men present smoke, but never use matches. Their cigarettes must be lighted only at the sacred fire.

After the days of preparation in this punctilious spot, the scalp-takers and other warriors emerge to hold the *T'u-a-fú-ar*, or "Mad Dance," in commemoration of their victory. The dance—which is never allowed to be witnessed by strangers—is held in a small square near the estufa. The dancers are formed in two lines, facing each other, with alternate men and women. The men are in their war paint, and each carries a bow and arrow in his left hand, and in his right a single arrow with the point upward. The women wear their gayest dresses and silver ornaments, but carry nothing in their hands. All the dancers move in perfect rhythm to the monotonous chant of the singers and the thump, thump of the big aboriginal drum. The chant is a metrical account of the battle and the manner in which the scalps were taken.

As soon as the dance is fairly under way, the "Bending Woman" makes her appearance. She is the official custodian of the scalps; has taken them from their sealed hiding-place in the estufa, and brushed them carefully with a sacred broom made in the mountains; and now carries them in a buckskin on her back, bending forward under the weight of their importance. As the dancers perform their evolutions she walks slowly and solemnly up and down between their lines with her precious burden.

This Mad Dance lasts four entire days. About seven o'clock on the evening of the last day comes *Khur-shú-ar*, the concluding Round Dance. A big bonfire is lighted, and the two parallel lines of dancers deploy around it until they form a large circle, the principal singers dropping out of the ranks, and clustering around the drummer beside the fire.

The song of the Round Dance is one of the prettiest of all sung by the Pueblos. It really is melodious and "catching." At the end of every phrase the effect is heightened by a chorus of high yells, in imitation of the war-whoop or "enemy-yell." Some of the older dancers, to whom the ceremony recalls real memories of their own, add doleful wails like those of the wounded. The whole performance is weird, but

21

not savage seeming. It has become merely a ritual—not a rehearsal of ferocity.

The chant and the dancing are kept up all night, until sunrise ends the celebration. All then repair to the estufa; the Bending Woman puts the scalps back in their niche, covers it with a flat slab of stone, and seals it over with mud.

The chief of the Cum-pa-huít-la-wen, after a solemn silence, says, " Brothers, friends, a road is given you " (that is, " You are free to depart "), and all file out, free to break their long abstinence, and enjoy themselves until the war-captain shall again summon them to the field.

Now that no fresh scalps have been acquired for so long, the old ones are still brought forth at a fixed time, and do duty, as the inspiration of the T'u-a-fú-ar. This dance, however, like many of the other old customs, is not so well kept up in Isleta as in some of the more remote pueblos which have not been so much affected by civilization. The T'u-a-fú-ar which I witnessed here in the fall of 1891 was the first the Isleteños had had in four years, though it should be held yearly. There was another in 1892.

XX.

DOCTORING THE YEAR.

ITH the Pueblo Indians the sick are not the only ones in need of doctoring. The medicine-men—those most important of Indian person-ages—have for patients not only sick people but well ones, and even the crops and the whole year's success. It would seem to a civilized physician a ridiculous affair to prescribe for the seasons and to feel the pulse of the corn-fields; but my aboriginal neighbors see no incongruity in it. On the contrary, they deem this profes-sional treatment of inanimate things as essential a matter as the care of the sick, and would have no hopes at all for the success of any year which was not duly provided for at the start by a most solemn dose of "medicine."

"Medicine" to an Indian has not merely the restricted sense in which we use it. *Wahr* (the word used by the Tig-uas) means almost every influence of every sort that affects the human race. The Indian has no idea of blind chance or unintelligent forces. To him everything is sentient; every influence which is agreeable in its effects is a good spirit or the work of a good spirit; and every influence which harms him is, or comes from, an evil spirit. All these influences are "medicines;" and so also, in a secondary sense, are the material agencies used to invoke or check them. The medicine-men, therefore, are people with supposed supernatural powers, who use good influences (either visible remedies or spiritual means) to bring welfare to the people and avert evil from them. A medicine-man has also power over the bad influences; but if he were to use that power to harm people he would be said to "have the evil road," and would be regarded no longer as a medicine-man, but as a witch—for the obligation to do good deeds only is doubly strong upon those who have powers not given to other men.

There are in the pueblo of Isleta countless medicine-makings, little and great, general and special; but the two most important ones of the year are the Spring Medicine-Making (or Medicine-Dance, as it is often called) to make the season prosperous, and the Medicine-Dance of thanksgiving to the good spirits, after the fall crops are harvested.

The Spring Medicine-Making, which is called in this language *Tu-sheé-wim*, is held generally about the middle of March, when the mild winter of the Rio Grande valley is practically done, and it is time to begin opening the great irrigating ditches, and other spring work. Every smallest detail is conducted with the utmost secrecy; and gentle as these people are, the safety of an American who should be caught spying upon any of these secrets would be very small indeed. For personal reasons it is impossible for me to divulge how I learned the following facts, but I can personally vouch for all of them.

When it is felt to be time to forecast and propitiate the year, the first step in the matter is taken by the Chief Captain of War and his seven sub-captains. They come together at his house; and he sends out the sub-captains to notify all the different branches of medicine-men—of which there are many. Each branch of medicine sends a delegate to the meeting, which proceeds to consider the best manner of taking the first formal step—the presentation of the sacred corn-meal to the Káh-ahm Ch'oóm-nin, the two Heads of All Medicine. The matter is fully discussed, and is finally put to vote of the meeting. As a rule the Chief Captain of War is chosen for this most important mission—unless he chances to be very ignorant of the necessary ceremonial songs, in which rare event one of the sub-captains is selected.

On the day after this meeting—which can be held only after sundown—the chosen war-captain, with his associate next in rank, must perform the errand. During the day the wife, mother, or sister of the senior of them carefully selects the best ears from her store of corn, and in a dark room grinds a handful into meal, on the metate (stone hand-mill), all the time praying that the errand of the sacred meal may be successful.

After sundown the ambassador wraps this bit of meal carefully in a clean square of corn-husk, and ties the packet with a corn-husk string. With this in his right hand he walks gravely to the house of the Head of All Medicine.

There are two of these dignitaries in this pueblo, one representing the Isleteños proper, and the other the Queres* colony here. They always begin as members of some special medicine order, but are promoted by degrees, until they leave their original orders altogether and become the two general and supreme heads of all the orders. To only one of these —the "Father of Here"—does the embassy go.

Entering the house, the bearer of the meal and his assistant sit down by the fire with the Father of Here, smoke the sacred cigarette to ward off evil spirits, and talk awhile on general matters. After a cigarette or two, the visitors rise and pray to the Trues on all sides to grant them success. The Father of Here of course knows all the time what is coming, but pretends not to hear them at all. Having finished their prayers, they turn to address him directly, telling him he is desired to make Tu-sheé-wim (medicine "for all the village"), to see if the year will be good, and to drive away evil spirits. Then the senior captain hands him the packet of sacred meal, which is always proffered and taken with the right hand only. For either of them to use the left hand in this (or any other) ceremonial would be sure death! As long as the visitors remain, the Father of Here must hold the meal in his hand. After they are gone, he walks to the house of the Father of the Queres and shares it with him — unless it is already too late at night, in which case he does not go until after sundown the next day.

The morning after both the Heads of All Medicine have

* Pronounced *Káy-ress.*

the sacred meal, they meet before sunrise at a point in the sand-hills east of the river. As the sun comes up over the Eagle Feather Mountains, they pray to the Sun-Father long and earnestly. Each now holds the sacred meal in his left hand, and each as he invokes some blessing on the people takes with his right hand a little pinch of the meal, breathes on it and tosses it toward the sun, until the meal is all gone. They pray that the Trues will send abundant rain, make the crops large, give plenty of grass for the herds, send good health to the village, etc. And when the meal has all been blown away, they return to the village and summon together their respective original medicine orders. With this morning begin the eight days of abstinence, purification, and preparation for the great event. Only the two special branches of medicine-men have to keep this ceremonial. The first four days are the "Outside Days," when the medicine-men may move about the pueblo and visit friends, but must keep their special fast. Then come the four "Inside Days," and with the beginning of these the medicine-men enter the medicine-house. There each is given a special seat, from which he must not move until the four days are over. In front of each stands a *tinaja* (jar) of water ; and he may drink as much as he chooses, but must not touch a mouthful of food in all those days, nor must a ray of sunlight strike him. The Common Mother, *Kai-íd-deh*, the wife of the Head of All Medicine, is the only other soul who can enter that solemn room ; and she sweeps it, brings them water and tobacco for cigarettes, and a sacred coal to light them. Day and night the fasters sit and smoke, the older men rehearsing the traditions of the order for the benefit of the younger, who must learn all these stories by heart. During all this time, no other person dare even call at the door. At about ten o'clock in the morning of the fourth Inside Day, any Americans or other strangers who may chance to be in town are sent out or shut up under a good-natured but inflexible sentinel. Then the coast is clear for the Cum-pa-huít-la-wen. Four pairs of these marshals are sent out, one pair to each cardinal point. In passing through the village they wear blankets, but once outside, cast these off and go running swiftly, clad only in their moccasins and the breech-clout. Besides their inseparable bows and arrows—the insignia of their office— each pair of guards carries a single "prayer-stick" which has been made that morning by the Head of All Medicine. This prayer-stick is a bit of wood about the size of a lead-pencil, with certain magical feathers bound to it in a certain way, varying according to the object to be prayed for.

The guards carry these prayer-sticks a long distance, plant them upright in some lonely and sheltered spot east, north, west, and south of the village, pray over them, and then set out on a long, wild run across country. At last they return to town across the fields and gardens (for these Indians are most industrious farmers) "blowing away the witches." Each guard carries a long feather in either hand, and as he runs homeward he is continually crossing these and snapping one over the other—which is supposed to toss up all evil spirits so that the winds will bear them away.

The medicine-making (or "dance") begins about eight o'clock that evening in the room where the fasters have kept their Inside Days. Before the doors are opened, the medicine-men remove their ordinary garments—for medicine-making must be done with only the dark-blue breech-clout —and paint their faces with *yeso* (a dingy whitewash made from gypsum) and *almagre* (a red mineral paint). The Father of All Medicine is marked with the *yeso* print of a bare hand on the outside of each thigh, and on the chest; and the two medicine-men who are to be the first performers—always the two who have last been received into the order—are indicated by *yeso* lightnings on their legs, as a symbol that they are the forerunners.

When the door is opened, the people outside remove their moccasins and stand motionless. The medicine-men sing, and the Father of All Medicine goes out to the public. Then he chooses the principal man of them all—always the cacique if that functionary is present—turns his back to him, and puts the tips of the eagle-feathers he carries back over his own shoulders. The cacique takes these tips in his hands, and is thus led into the room followed in single file by the people. He is given the "seat of honor" nearest the medicine-men; and the general public seats itself at will outside a line which has been drawn on the adobe floor about ten feet in front of the medicine-men, sitting only on moccasins and blankets. The shamans are seated in a semicircle, facing the public. The Father of All Medicine sits in the center, and the rest are ranged on either side of him in the order of their rank, so that the two men at the ends of the semi-circle are the newest in the order. In front of each medi-cine-man is the sacred "Mother," the chief implement of all medicine-branches—a flawless ear of white corn, with a tuft of downy feathers at the top, and turquoise ornaments.* And in front of the Father of All Medicine is the *cajete* (earthen bowl) of sacred water, in whose clear bosom he can see all that is going on in the world!

When the public is seated, the medicine-men sing a sacred song to make the people center their thoughts on nothing but the matter in hand. The English of this song would be about as follows:

> Now bring the Corn, Our Mother,
> And all the common corn;
> In all our thoughts and words
> Let us do only good;
> In all our acts and words
> Let us be all as one.

While this song is being sung over several times, the two youngest medicine-men rise from their seats on the floor, and step to where a bowl of sacred corn-meal stands before the Father of All Medicine. Here they stand and pray, at each request picking up a pinch of the meal and blowing part of it toward the Father of All Medicine and part toward the Mother-Corn. Then they go down the aisle, which is kept open, to the door, crossing and snapping their eagle-feathers to toss up and blow away any evil thought that may be in the crowd. By the time they return to the open space the song

* The emblem of the soul.

is ended and another is begun; and now the next youngest
pair of medicine-men rise and join the first, going through
the same performance. This is kept up till nearly all the
medicine-men are on their feet together. Then begins the
wonderful sleight of hand, which is the most startling feature
of all, and the one which maintains the superstitious power
of the shamans over their people. It is described in another
chapter. This conjuring, which is the "Medicine-Dance"
proper, continues through five songs. Then the performers
take their seats for a rest, and smoke cigarettes which the
Cum-pa-huít-la-wen roll for them, and presently rise to resume their magic.

When this medicine-making is done—which is only when
all present are cured of all their real or imaginary diseases
—comes the equally important *Ta-win-kóor-shahn-mée-ee*, the
sacred "going-out-for-the-year." The Father of All Medicine
rises, with the two next in rank to himself, and dances awhile.
Then he puts on his left hand and arm a great glove of the
skin of a bear's fore-leg, with the claws on; and upon each
foot a similar boot from the bear's hind-leg. In the glove he
sticks his eagle-feathers; but his two assistants, who do not
have the bear-trappings, carry their feathers in their hands.
While these three shamans stand in a row before the assemblage, the others sing for them a special song:

> Ai-ay, ai-ay, hyah ay-ah
> Ay-ah, ay-ah, ay-ah!
>
> After the Sun-Father
> We will follow, follow, follow!

When this song is sung a second time, the Father of All Medicine goes behind his two assistants and looks in the sacred *cajete*, to find if it be time to go out. Seeing that it is, he starts on a half-run to the door, followed by the two others. There are always two Cum-pa-huít-la-wen at the door, and one of these accompanies the three shamans. They go to a certain point on the bank of the Rio Grande, and there receive the omens which they declare the river brings down to them from its source in the home of the Trues of the North. Among these tokens are always bunches of green blades of corn and wheat—many weeks before a spear of either cereal is growing out-of-doors within hundreds of miles of here. Last year "the river brought them" also a live rabbit—which is much more easily accounted for —as a sign that it would be a good year for game.

Returning with these articles, they enter the medicine-house, and show them to the whole assemblage. If the leaves are green and lusty, it will be a good year for crops; but if they are yellow, there will be a drought. Then the three " Goers-Out " lay the articles before their medicine-seats and sit down for a rest.

Then the medicine-making song is resumed, and the conjuring begins again, and is kept up almost all night.

After a possible witch-chase (described in another chapter) comes the sacred water-giving. The two youngest shamans take the *cajetes* and carry them before the crowd. To each person they give a mouthful, praying the Trues to give him a clean heart, strength, and health. The recipient does not swallow all the water, but blows a little on his hands and rubs it upon his body, believing that it will give him strength.

After all have had the sacred water, the next ceremony is the *Ká-kee-roon*, the "Mother-Shaking." The Father of All Medicine takes up all the (corn) "Mothers," two at a time, and shakes them over the heads of the seated audience, raining a shower of seeds. The people eagerly scramble for these seeds, for it is firmly believed that he who puts even one of them with his spring planting will secure a very large crop.

All the audience who desire now go in front of the semicircle of seated medicine-men and pray, scattering the sacred corn-meal on the row of "Mothers." Then all sing a long song, of which the verse has the following meaning:

> Now! Now!
> Our Mother, Corn Mother!
> Her Sun is coming up!
> Our Mother, Corn Mother!
> Her Sun is arriving!
> Our Mother, Corn Mother!
> Her Sun is entering!
> She is the one who
> Gives us the road.
> She is the one who
> Makes the road.
> She is the one who
> Points the road to us!

This song is a sort of benediction, and is sung standing. It is begun when the morning sun is really coming up behind the mountains, and the Father of All Medicine can no longer delay to "give them the road"—that is, dismiss the

22

meeting.   He rises and prays to the Trues to bless all present and those who were unable to attend, and to crown the year with success to all.   Then he says: "A road is given you," and the people all file out, and when once outside put on their moccasins and hurry home.

After they are gone, all the women bring to the door offerings of food, which are set before the medicine-men by the Common Mother, and they eat heartily after their long and trying fast.   What is left is divided among them to be taken home.   Having eaten and smoked, the medicine-men wash off the ceremonial paint, resume their ordinary clothing, close the medicine-house, and return to their homes.   That is the end of the *Tu-sheé-wim*, and the year is now supposed to be safely started toward a successful issue—which will largely depend, however, upon later and special medicine-makings for special occasions and emergencies.

XXI.

N this view of the Strange Corners we ought certainly to include a glimpse at the home-life of the Pueblos. A social organization which looks upon children as belonging to the mother and not to the father; which makes it absolutely imperative that husband and wife shall be of different divisions of society; which makes it impossible for a man to own a house, and gives every woman entire control of her home—with many other equally remarkable points of etiquette—is surely different from what most of us are used to. But in the neglected corners of our own country there are ten thousand citizens of the United States to whom these curious arrangements are endeared by the customs of immemorial centuries.

The basis of society in the twenty-six quaint town-republics of the Pueblos—communities which are by far the most peaceful and the best-governed in North America—is not the family, as with us, but the clan. These clans are clusters of families—arbitrary social divisions, of which there are from

six to sixteen in each Pueblo town. In Isleta there are sixteen clans—the Sun People, the Earth People, the Water-
Pebble People, the Eagle People, the Mole People, the Antelope People, the Deer People, the Mountain-Lion People, the
Turquoise People, the Parrot People, the White Corn People,
the Red Corn People, the Blue Corn People, the Yellow Corn
People, the Goose People, and the Wolf People. Every Indian of the eleven hundred and fifty in the pueblo belongs
to one of these clans. A man of the Eagle People cannot
marry a woman of that clan, nor vice versa. Husband and
wife *must* be of different clans. Still odder is the law of descent. With us—and all civilized nations—descent is from
the father; but with the Pueblos, and nearly all aboriginal
peoples, it is from the mother. For instance, a man of the
Wolf Clan marries a woman of the Mole Clan. Their children belong not to the Wolf People but to the Mole People,
by birth. But if the parents do not personally like the head
man of that clan, they can have some friend adopt the children into the Sun or Earth or any other clan.

There are no *Indian* family names; but all the people here
have taken Spanish ones—and the children take the name of
their mother and not of their father. Thus, my landlady is
the wife of Antonio Jojola. Her own name is Maria Gracia
Chihuihui; and their roly-poly son—who is commonly known
as Juan Gordo, "Fat John," or, as often, since I once photographed him crawling out of an adobe oven, as Juan Biscocho,
"John Biscuit"—is Juan Chihuihui. If he grows up to
marry and have children, they will not be Chihuihuis nor Jo-

jolas, but will bear the Spanish last name of his wife. This pueblo, however, is changing from the old customs more than are any of the other towns; and in some families the children are divided, the sons bearing the father's name, and the daughters the mother's. In their own language, each Indian has a single name, which belongs to him or her alone, and is never changed.

The Pueblos almost without exception now have their children baptized in a Christian church and given a Spanish name. But those who are "True Believers" in "the Ways of the Old" have also an Indian christening. Even as I write, scores of dusky, dimpled babes in this pueblo are being given strange Tigua names by stalwart godfathers, who hold them up before the line of dancers who celebrate the spring opening of the great main irrigating-ditch. Here the christening is performed by a friend of the family, who takes the babe to the dance, selects a name, and seals it by putting his lips to the child's lips.* In some pueblos this office is performed by the nearest woman-friend of the mother. She takes the child from the house at dawn on the third day after its birth, and names it after the first object that meets her eye after the sun comes up. Sometimes it is Bluish-Light-of-Dawn, sometimes Arrow-(ray)of-the-Sun, sometimes Tall-Broken-Pine—

* My own little girl, born in the pueblo of Isleta, was formally christened by an Indian friend, one day, and has ever since been known to the Indians as T'hur-be-sáy, "the Rainbow of the Sun." For a month after her birth they came daily to see her, bringing little gifts of silver, calico, chocolate, eggs, Indian pottery, and the like, as is one of their customs.

and so on.   It is this custom which gives rise to many of the
Indian names which seem so odd to us.

When a child is born in a Pueblo town, a curious duty
devolves upon the father.   For the next eight days he must
keep a fire going—no matter what the weather—in the
quaint little *fogon* or adobe fireplace, and see that it never
goes out by day or night.   This sacred birth-fire can be kindled only in the religious wáys—by the fire-drill, flint and
steel, or by a brand from the hearth of the cacique.   If pater-
familias is so unlucky as to let the birth-fire go out, there is
but one thing for him to do.   Wrapping his blanket around
him, he stalks solemnly to the house of the cacique, enters,
and seats himself on the floor by the hearth—for the cacique
must *always* have a fire.   He dare not ask for what he wants;
but making a cigarette, he lights it at the coals and improves
the opportunity to smuggle a living coal under his blanket
—generally in no better receptacle than his own tough, bare
hand.   In a moment he rises, bids the cacique good-by, and
hurries home, carefully nursing the sacred spark, and with it
he rekindles the birth-fire.   It is solemnly believed that if this
fire were relighted in any other manner, the child would not
live out the year.

The Pueblo men—contrary to the popular idea about all
Indians—take a very generous share in caring for their
children.   When they are not occupied with the duties of
busy farmers, then fathers, grandfathers, and great-grand-
fathers are generally to be seen each with a fat infant slung
in the blanket on his back, its big eyes and plump face peep-

ing over his shoulder. The white-haired Governor, the stern-faced War-Captain, the grave *Principales*—none of them are too dignified to "tote" the baby up and down the courtyard or to the public square and to solemn dances; or even to dance a remarkable domestic jig, if need be, to calm a squall from the precious riders upon their backs.

A Pueblo town is the children's paradise. The parents are fairly ideal in their relations to their children. They are uniformly gentle, yet never foolishly indulgent. A Pueblo child is almost never punished, and almost never needs to be. Obedience and respect to age are born in these brown young Americans, and are never forgotten by them. I never saw a "spoiled child" in all my long acquaintance with the Pueblos.

The Pueblo woman is absolute owner of the house and all that is in it, just as her husband owns the fields which he tills. He is a good farmer and she a good housewife. Fields and rooms are generally models of neatness.

The Pueblos marry under the laws of the church; but many of them add a strange ceremony of their own—which was their custom when Columbus discovered America. The betrothed couple are given two ears of raw corn; to the youth a blue ear, but to the maiden a white one, because her heart is supposed to be whiter. They must prove their devotion by eating the very last hard kernel. Then they run a sacred foot-race in presence of the old councilors. If the girl comes in ahead, she "wins a husband" and has a little ascendancy over him; if he comes in first to the goal, he "wins a wife."

If the two come in together, it is a bad omen, and the match is declared off.

Pueblo etiquette as to the acquaintance of young people is extremely strict. No youth and maiden must walk or talk together; and as for a visit or a private conversation, both the offenders—no matter how mature—would be soundly whipped by their parents. Acquaintance between young people before marriage is limited to a casual sight of each other, a shy greeting as they pass, or a word when they meet in the presence of their elders. Matches are not made by the parents, as was the case with their Mexican neighbors until very recently—and as it still is in many European countries —but marriages are never against the parental consent. When a boy wishes to marry a certain girl, the parents conduct all the formal "asking for" her and other preliminaries.

The very curious division of the sexes which the Spanish found among the Pueblos three hundred and fifty years ago has now almost entirely disappeared—as have also the community-houses which resulted from the system. In old times only the women, girls, and young children lived in the dwellings. The men and boys slept always in the estufa. Thither their wives and mothers brought their meals, themselves eating with the children at home. So there was no family home-life, and never was until the brave Spanish missionaries gradually brought about a change to the real home that the Indians so much enjoy to-day.

When an Indian dies, there are many curious ceremonials besides the attempts to throw the witches off the track of his spirit. Food must be provided for the soul's four days' journey; and property must also be sent on to give the deceased " a good start " in the next world. If the departed was a man and had horses and cattle, some of them are killed that he may have them in the Beyond. His gun, his knife, his bow and arrows, his dancing-costume, his clothing, and other personal property are also " killed " (in the Indian phrase), by burning or breaking them; and by this means he is supposed to have the use of them again in the other world—where he will eat and hunt and dance and farm just as he has done here. In the vicinity of every Pueblo town is always a "killing-place "—entirely distinct and distant from the consecrated graveyard where the body is laid—and there the ground is strewn with countless broken weapons and ornaments, earthen jars, stone hand-mills, and other utensils— for when a woman dies, her household furniture is " sent on " after her in the same fashion. The precious beads of coral, turquoise, and silver, and the other silver jewelry, of which these people have great quantities, is generally laid away with the body in the bare, brown graveyard in front of the great adobe church.

XXII.

A SAINT IN COURT.

HILE law in the abstract may deserve its reputation as one of the driest of subjects, the history of its development, provisions, and applications contains much that is curious and interesting. There have been, among different nations and in different ages, laws remarkable for eccentricity; and as for the astonishing causes in which the aid of justice has been invoked, a mere catalogue of them would be of appalling length. Nor are these legal curiosities confined to bygone ages and half-civilized nations. Our own country has furnished laws and lawsuits perhaps as remarkable as any.

Among these suits, none is more interesting than one of the few legal contests in which the Pueblo Indians have ever figured. With these quiet, decorous, kind, and simple-hearted children of the Sun, quarrels of any sort are extremely rare, and legal controversies still rarer; but there was one lawsuit between two of the principal Pueblo towns which excited great interest among all the Indians and Mexicans of the territory, and the few Saxon-Americans who were then here; which

nearly made a war—a lawsuit for a saint! It was finally ad-
judicated by the Supreme Court of New Mexico in January,
1857. It figures in the printed reports of that high tribunal,
under the title, "The Pueblo of Laguna *vs.* The Pueblo of
Acoma"—being an appeal in the case of Acoma *vs.* Laguna.

Of all the nineteen pueblos of New Mexico, Acoma is by
far the most wonderful. Indeed, it is probably the most remarkable city in the world. Perched upon the level summit
of a great "box" of rock whose perpendicular sides are nearly
four hundred feet high, and reached by some of the dizziest
paths ever trodden by human feet, the prehistoric town looks
far across the wilderness. Its quaint terraced houses of gray
adobe, its huge church—hardly less wonderful than the pyramids of Egypt as a monument of patient toil—its great
reservoir in the solid rock, its superb scenery, its romantic
history, and the strange customs of its six hundred people,
all are rife with interest to the few Americans who visit the
isolated city. Neither history nor tradition tells us when
Acoma was founded. The pueblo was once situated on top
of the Mesa Encantada (Enchanted Table-land), which rises
seven hundred feet in air near the mesa now occupied. Four
hundred years ago or so, a frightful storm swept away the
enormous leaning rock which served as a ladder, and the
patient people—who were away at the time—had to build a
new city. The present Acoma was an old town when the first
European—Coronado, the famous Spanish explorer—saw it
in 1540. With that its authentic history begins—a strange,
weird history, in scattered fragments, for which we must

delve among the curious "memorials" of the Spanish conquerors and the scant records of the heroic priests.

Laguna lies about twenty miles northeast of Acoma, and
is now a familiar sight to travelers on the A. & P. R. R.,
which skirts the base of the sloping rock on which the town
is built. It is a much younger town than Acoma, of which
it is a daughter colony, but has a half more people. It was
founded in 1699.

One of the notable things about the venerable Catholic
churches of New Mexico is the number of ancient paintings
and statues of the saints which they contain. Some are the
rude daubs on wood made by devout Indians, and some are
the canvases of prominent artists of Mexico and Spain. It
was concerning one of the latter that the curious lawsuit between Laguna and Acoma arose.

There is considerable mystery concerning this picture,
arising from the lack of written history. The painting of
San José* (St. Joseph) was probably the one presented by
Charles II. of Spain. Entregas, in his "Visits," enumer-
ates the pictures which he found in the Laguna church in
1773, and mentions among them "a canvas of a yard and a
half, with the most holy likeness of St. Joseph with his blue
mark, the which was presented by Our Lord the King."
The Acomas, however, claim that the king gave the picture
to them originally, and there is no doubt that it was in their
possession over a hundred years ago.

When brave Fray Ramirez founded his lonely mission in

* Pronounced *Sahn Ho-záy.*

Acoma in 1629, he dedicated the little adobe chapel "To God, to the Holy Catholic Church, and to St. Joseph." San José was the patron saint of the pueblo, and when the fine Spanish painting of him was hung on the dull walls of a later church, it became an object of peculiar veneration to the simple natives. Their faith in it was touching. Whether it was that the attacks of the merciless Apache might be averted, or that a pestilence might be checked, or that their crops might be abundant, it was to San José that they went with prayers and votive offerings. And as generation after generation was born, lived its quaint life, and was at last laid to rest in the wonderful graveyard, the veneration of the painting grew stronger and more clear, while oil and canvas were growing dim and moldy.

Many years ago — we do not know the date — the people of Laguna found themselves in a very bad way. Several successive crops had failed them, winter storms had wrought havoc to house and farm, and a terrible epidemic had carried off scores of children. And all this time Acoma was prospering wonderfully. Acoma believed it was because of San José; and Laguna began to believe so too. At last the governor and principal men of Laguna, after solemn council, mounted their silver-trapped ponies, wrapped their costliest blankets about them, and rode over valley and mesa to "the City in the Sky." A runner had announced their coming, and they were formally received by the *principales* of Acoma, and escorted to the dark estufa. After a propitiatory smoke the Laguna spokesman began the speech. They all knew

23

how his pueblo had suffered, while Laguna had no saint on whom they could rely. It was now the first of March. Holy Week was almost here, and Laguna desired to celebrate it with unusual ceremonies, hoping thereby to secure divine favor. Would Acoma kindly lend San José to her sister pueblo for a season, that he might bring his blessing to the afflicted town?

A white-headed Acoma replied for his people. They knew how angry *Tata Dios* had been with Laguna, and wished to help appease him if possible. Acoma needed San José's presence in Holy Week; but she was prosperous and would do without him. She would lend him to Laguna for a month, but then he must be returned without fail.

So next day, when the Laguna delegation started homeward, two strong men carried the precious canvas carefully between them, and that night it hung upon the rudely decorated walls of the Laguna church, while hundreds of solemn Indians knelt before it. And in the procession of Holy Week it was borne in a little shrine about the town while its escort fired their rusty flint-locks in reiterant salute.

Old men tell me that there was a change in the fortunes of Laguna from that day forth. At all events, when the month was up the Lagunas did not return the borrowed painting, and the Acoma messengers who came next day to demand it were informed that it would stay where it was unless Acoma could take it by force of arms. The Acomas then appealed to their priest, Fray Mariano de Jesus Lopez, the last of the Franciscans here. He cited the *principales* of both pueblos to appear before him in Acoma on a certain day, bringing the saint.

When they were all assembled there, the priest ordered a season of prayer that God and San José would see justice done in the matter at issue, and after this held mass. He then suggested that they draw lots for the saint, to which both pueblos cordially agreed, believing that God would direct the result. It was a solemn and impressive sight when all were gathered in the great, gloomy church. Near the altar was a *tinaja* (earthen jar) covered with a white cloth. At each side stood a wee Acoma girl dressed in spotless white, from the paño over her shoulders to the queer, boot-like buckskin leggings. Beside one of them was the old priest, who acted for Acoma; and beside the other were Luis Saraceno and Margarita Hernandez, on behalf of Laguna. Twelve ballots were put in the *tinaja* and well shaken; eleven were blank, the twelfth had a picture of the saint rudely drawn upon it.

"Draw," said Fray Mariano, when all was ready; and Maria thrust her little arm into the jar and drew out a ballot, which she handed to the priest. "Acoma, blank! Draw, Lolita, for Laguna." Lolita dived down and drew a blank also. Maria drew the third ballot, and Lolita the fourth — both blanks. And then a devout murmur ran through the gathered Acomas as Maria drew forth the fifth paper, which bore the little picture of San José.

"God has decided in favor of Acoma," said the priest, "and San José stays in his old home." The crowd poured out of the church, the Acomas hugging each other and thanking God, the Lagunas walking surlily away.

Such a feast had never been in Acoma as the grateful people began to prepare; but their rejoicing was short-lived. That very evening a strong armed force of Lagunas came quietly up the great stone "ladder" to the lofty town, and appeared suddenly in front of the church. "Open the door," they said to the frightened sacristan, "or we will break it down. We have come for the saint." The news ran through the little town like wild-fire. All Acoma was wild with grief and rage; and hopeless as a war with Laguna would have been, it would have commenced then and there but for the counsel of the priest. He exhorted his flock to avoid bloodshed and give the saint up to the Lagunas, leaving a final decision of the dispute to the courts. His advice prevailed; and after a few hours of excitement the Lagunas departed with their precious booty.

As soon thereafter as the machinery of the law could be set in motion, the Pueblos of Acoma filed in the District Court of the Second Judicial District of New Mexico a bill of Chancery *vs.* the Pueblo of Laguna, setting forth the above facts in detail.

They also asked that a receiver be appointed to take charge of San José till the matter should be decided. The Lagunas promptly filed an answer setting forth that they knew nothing of Acoma's claim that the picture was originally given to Acoma; that by their own traditions it was clearly the property of Laguna, and that Acoma stole it; that they went peaceably to reclaim it, and Acoma refused to give it up; that Acoma proposed to draw lots for it, but they refused and took it home.

Judge Kirby Benedict, sitting as chancellor, heard this extraordinary case, and the evidence being overwhelmingly in favor of Acoma, decided accordingly. The Lagunas appealed to the Supreme Court, which after most careful investigation affirmed the decision of the chancellor. In rendering his decision the judge said:

"Having disposed of all the points, . . . the court deems it not improper to indulge in some reflections on this interesting case. The history of this painting, its obscure origin, its age, and the fierce contest which these two Indian pueblos have carried on, bespeak the inappreciable value which is placed upon it. The intrinsic value of the oil, paint, and cloth by which San José is represented to the senses, it has been admitted in argument, probably would not exceed twenty-five cents; but this seemingly worthless painting has well-nigh cost these two pueblos a bloody and cruel struggle, and had it not been for weakness on the part of one of the pueblos, its history might have been written in blood. . . . One witness swore that unless San José is in Acoma, the people cannot prevail with God. All these supposed virtues and attributes pertaining to this saint, and the belief that the throne of God can be successfully approached only through him, have contributed to make this a case of deep interest, involving a portraiture of the feelings, passions, and character of these peculiar people. Let the decree below be affirmed."

This settled the matter, and Acoma sent a delegation to take the saint to his home. Half-way to Laguna they found the painting resting against a tree beside the road, the face toward Acoma. To this day the simple people believe that San José knew he was now free, and was in such haste to get back to Acoma that he started out by himself! The dim and tattered canvas hangs beside the altar in the great church at Acoma still, and will so long as a shred is left.

Fray Mariano, who thus averted a destructive war, met a tragic end in 1848. He went out one morning to shoot a chicken for dinner. His venerable pistol would not work till he looked into it to see what was the matter. Then it went off and blew out his brains.

These are a few of the Strange Corners of our own country. There are very many more, of which others can tell you much better than I. This book is meant to call your attention chiefly to the southwest, which is the most remarkable area in the United States and the most neglected—though by no means the only one worth learning about and seeing. The whole West is full of wonders, and we need not run to other lands to gratify our longing for the curious and the wonderful. The trip abroad may at least be postponed until we are ready to tell those we shall meet in foreign lands something of the wonders of our own.